I0426253

Maine Appalachian Trail Rare Mammal Inventory from 2006-2008

Natural Resource Report NPS/NETN/NRR—2010/177

David Yates, Sarah Folsom, and David Evers

BioDiversity Research Institute
19 Flaggy Meadow Rd
Gorham, Maine 04038

February 2010

U.S. Department of the Interior
National Park Service
Natural Resource Program Center
Fort Collins, Colorado

The National Park Service, Natural Resource Program Center publishes a range of reports that address natural resource topics of interest and applicability to a broad audience in the National Park Service and others in natural resource management, including scientists, conservation and environmental constituencies, and the public.

The Natural Resource Report Series is used to disseminate high-priority, current natural resource management information with managerial application. The series targets a general, diverse audience, and may contain NPS policy considerations or address sensitive issues of management applicability.

All manuscripts in the series receive the appropriate level of peer review to ensure that the information is scientifically credible, technically accurate, appropriately written for the intended audience, and designed and published in a professional manner. This report received formal peer review by subject-matter experts who were not directly involved in the collection, analysis, or reporting of the data, and whose background and expertise put them on par technically and scientifically with the authors of the information.

Views, statements, findings, conclusions, recommendations, and data in this report are those of the author(s) and do not necessarily reflect views and policies of the National Park Service, U.S. Department of the Interior. Mention of trade names or commercial products does not constitute endorsement or recommendation for use by the National Park Service.

This report is also available from the Northeast Temperate Network Inventory & Monitoring program website (http://science.nature.nps.gov/im/units/netn/) and the Natural Resource Publications Management website (http://www.nature.nps.gov/publications/NRPM).

Please cite this publication as:

Yates, D., S. Folsom, and D. Evers. 2010. Maine Appalachian Trail rare mammal inventory from 2006-2008. Natural Resource Report NPS/NETN/NRR—2010/177. National Park Service, Fort Collins, Colorado.

NPS 962/101073 February 2010

Contents

Figures

Tables

Executive Summary

A primary objective of the National Park Service (NPS) Inventory & Monitoring (I&M) program is to document 90% of the vertebrates and vascular plants within a park's boundaries using existing verifiable data (e.g., voucher specimens) and field investigations. While detailed biological inventories have been carried out in several National Parks and National Forests associated with the Appalachian National Scenic Trail (A.T.) corridor, relatively few inventories have been conducted on A.T. lands outside these areas. Because 1,045 of the 2,100 A.T. miles (~50%) are outside National Parks or National Forests, inventories such as the one conducted in Maine that targets lands administered directly by the Appalachian Trail Park Office holds are necessary.

We conducted an inventory that focused on expanding knowledge of at-risk small mammal species identified during prior natural heritage inventory work. The areas of concern were those parts of the A.T. corridor in Maine that includes the western mountains and central highland regions. The primary objective of the inventory was to determine whether each target species was present along the designated section of the A.T. We attempted to sample and identify the presence of as many species as possible with the goal of sampling those mammal species considered rare and high priority by state and federal entities. The hope is that this information will be used to develop monitoring and management strategies as well as contribute to the development of a long-term monitoring program for rare species along the A.T. in Maine.

In 2006, we surveyed 10 sites along the A. T. for the presence of three target small mammal species: the northern bog lemming (*Synaptomys borealis*), yellow-nosed or rock vole (*Microtus chrotorrhinus*), and the long-tailed or rock shrew (*Sorex dispar*). We sampled a total of 2997 trap nights. Two rock voles were captured at two study locations in Crocker and Bigelow Mountains. A meadow vole (*Microtus pennsylvanicus*) was captured at a third study site, Saddleback Mountain. Meadow voles are rarely found at high elevations in areas with continuous forests, making this finding noteworthy.

Also in 2006, we surveyed seven sites along the A.T. for the presence of the eastern small-footed bat (*Myotis leibii*). We used a combination of mist nets and ultra-sonic bat detectors (Sonobat) to determine the presence of several species at each study site. We detected six species along the corridor. The most common was the little brown bat (*Myotis lucifugus*) followed by the northern long-eared bat (*Myotis septentrionalis*). Other species found were the big brown bat (*Eptesicus fuscus*), hoary bat (*Lasiurus cinereus*), red bat (*Lasiurus borealis*), and silver-haired bat (*Lasionycteris noctivagans*).While we did not detect/capture any eastern small-footed bats, the red, hoary, and silver-haired bats are considered noteworthy due to their association with contiguous forests and because information on the these three species in Maine is lacking.

The Maine Department of Inland Fisheries and Wildlife (MEDIF&W) has on-going inventories for the Canada lynx (*Lynx Canadensis*) in Maine and has developed specific snow-tracking protocols for this species. We followed their protocol to determine the presence of Canada lynx along the A.T. corridor. Surveys began 24 hours after a snow event, the period considered to provide the best conditions for winter tracking. Nine townships along the A.T. were surveyed for lynx in the winter months from January through March in 2007 and 2008. There was a total of eight sets of lynx tracks observed in three townships including: Elliotsville Township, T2R10, and T7R9NWP. Several other mammal species were observed during tracking. We recorded 27 individual pine marten (*Martes martes*), 10 fisher (*Martes penannti*), and four river otter (*Lontra canadensis*). We observed pine marten in all but one township (Elliotsville), with fisher and river otter occurring in four out of 10 townships. A less common presence was the bobcat (*Lynx rufus*), with only one individual observed in the Elliotsville Township.

Small Mammal Survey

Introduction

A primary objective of the National Park Service (NPS) Inventory & Monitoring (I&M) program is to document 90% of the vertebrates and vascular plants within a park's boundaries using existing verifiable data (e.g., voucher specimens) and field investigations. While detailed biological inventories have been carried out in several National Parks and National Forests associated with the Appalachian National Scenic Trail (A.T.) corridor, relatively few inventories have been conducted on A.T. lands outside these existing Federal lands. Because approximately 1,045 of the 2,100 A.T. miles (~50%) are outside National Parks or National Forests, inventories such as the one conducted in Maine that targets lands administered directly by the Appalachian Trail Park Office holds are necessary.

In 2006, we conducted a small mammal survey along the Maine portion of the A.T. The goal of the survey was to document the presence of several rare small mammals including: the northern bog lemming (*Synaptomys borealis*), yellow-nosed/rock vole (*Microtus chrotorrhinus*), long-tailed shrew (*Sorex dispar*), and the Gaspé shrew (*Sorex gaspensis*). All are state listed species of special concern in Maine and efforts to determine current distributions are considered important by both the state and the Appalachian Trail Park Office, and any detection of these target species would be a significant contribution to the continuing evaluation of their respective range and habitat associations. To date, the Maine Department of Inland Fisheries and Wildlife (MEDIF&W) has surveyed for these species, with limited success, as part of their ecoregion study at some sites along the A.T., including the Bigelow Mountains in western Maine. The rare small mammal species targeted by this study are sparsely distributed which makes determining their presence or absence difficult, therefore sampling a site multiple times is necessary to establish presence or absence.

Northern Bog Lemming

In Maine, the northern bog lemming is listed as threatened and is generally associated with high-elevation moist areas. Until recent years, it was documented only in Piscataquis County, initially at the tableland of Mt. Katahdin (Preble 1899). Clough and Albright (1987) validated its continuing presence there 90 years later and also collected the species at Nesowadnahunk Field Campground in a nearby, low-elevation setting in Baxter State Park. Ten years later, a northern bog lemming was caught in a moist *Sphagnum* patch at the top of Reddington Pond Range (MEDIF&W, Franklin County, S. Pelletier, pers. comm.). In 2001, a northern bog lemming was collected at Sweeny Pond and another collected at Gardner Mountain during a field effort by the MEDIF&W (Herrmann et al. 2003). Lastly, a northern bog lemming was collected at a low elevation site in the White Mountain National Forest, New Hampshire, approximately 4 km west of the Maine border (MEDIF&W, M. Yamasaki, pers. comm.).

Northern bog lemmings are habitat specialists typically found in moist, mossy areas at high elevation or latitude (Preble 1899, Osgood 1909, Wright 1950, Edwards 1963, Layser and Burke 1973, Wilson et al. 1980). Therefore we focused our survey efforts in these microhabitats along the A.T.

Yellow-nosed/rock vole

The yellow-nosed or rock vole is uncommon in Maine, and is listed as a species of special concern. Unlike the northern bog lemming, this species is not restricted to northern latitudes. Yellow-nosed voles range from Labrador and Quebec (Whitaker and Martin 1977) west to Minnesota (Timm et al. 1977) and south through Pennsylvania (Kirkland and Hart 1999) and West Virginia (Healy and Brooks 1988). There are 14 documented occurrences in Maine, mostly in the western mountains or the Baxter State Park vicinity in northern Maine. In 2001, the MEDIF&W collected three specimens of Yellow-nosed voles at Green Mountain, as well as one specimen each on Ironbound and Trickey Bluff mountains (Hermann et al. 2003). These individuals were collected in rocky areas, which have been deemed to be typical settings for rock voles. However, Buech et al. (1977) suggested certain microhabitat characteristics may be more important to yellow-nosed voles, including: a sparse overstory of trees, dense shrubs, sparse herb cover on the ground, and a thick layer of moist litter. Sites with abundant crevices beneath rocks and tree roots provide the best habitat. According to Kirkland and Knipe (1979), the yellow-nosed vole is not restricted to boreal, high-elevation rocky habitats, but may be found in the transition zone of northern hardwood species such as yellow birch (*Betula lutea*), sugar maple (*Acer saccharum*) and American beech (*Fagus grandifolia*). However, French and Crowell (1985) found significantly more yellow-nosed voles in spruce-fir habitats than in northern hardwood habitats in New York.

Long-tailed Shrew

Long-tailed shrews range from Maine and Quebec south along the Appalachian Mountains to North Carolina and Tennessee (Kirkland and van Duesen 1979). Habitats of long-tailed shrews have generally been described as talus slopes or boulder areas in deep woods at high elevations (French and Crowell 1985), or rocky, northern hardwood sites (Scott 1987, Woolaver et al. 1998). The species is often associated with a nearby stream or other source of water (Roscoe and Majka 1976, Woolaver et al. 1998).

Gaspé Shrew

The Gaspé shrew has a very restricted range, and is found primarily in Quebec. It was also detected in a few rocky areas amongst northern hardwood forests in Nova Scotia (Roscoe and Majka 1976) and New Brunswick (Whitaker and French 1984). The Gaspé shrew has never been documented in Maine, but has been found nearby in New Brunswick (Scott 1987) and could exist in little studied areas of adjacent northern Maine. Some researchers suggest that the Gaspé shrew and long-tailed shrew may be the same species (Kirkland and van Deusen 1979).

Study Area

Many of the target species are habitat specialists with spotty distributions. Accordingly, site selection along the A.T. targeted habitat areas associated with these species and was determined by known distribution records (e.g. MEDIF&W databases). We also chose sites based on habitat using GIS layers from the National Land Cover Dataset (NLCD 2001). For many taxa, we identified more study areas along the A.T. than logistical constraints would permit us to sample. Therefore, we determined a reasonable number of study areas for each target taxon based upon available time and personnel. For example, some potential areas were eliminated if they were very difficult to access.

Using the above protocol, we selected 10 sites for small mammals along the A.T. corridor (Figure 1). Study sites were generally at or above 2,500 feet, and were characterized by steep talus slopes (wooded or exposed) and/or moist locations with *Sphagnum* moss (Figure 2). However, not all sites were characterized by the presence of both talus slopes and *Sphagnum*, only one or the other. All study sites provided deep rock crevices for target species. One high elevation bog (Saddleback) was chosen based on the presence of deep, moist *Sphagnum* mats.

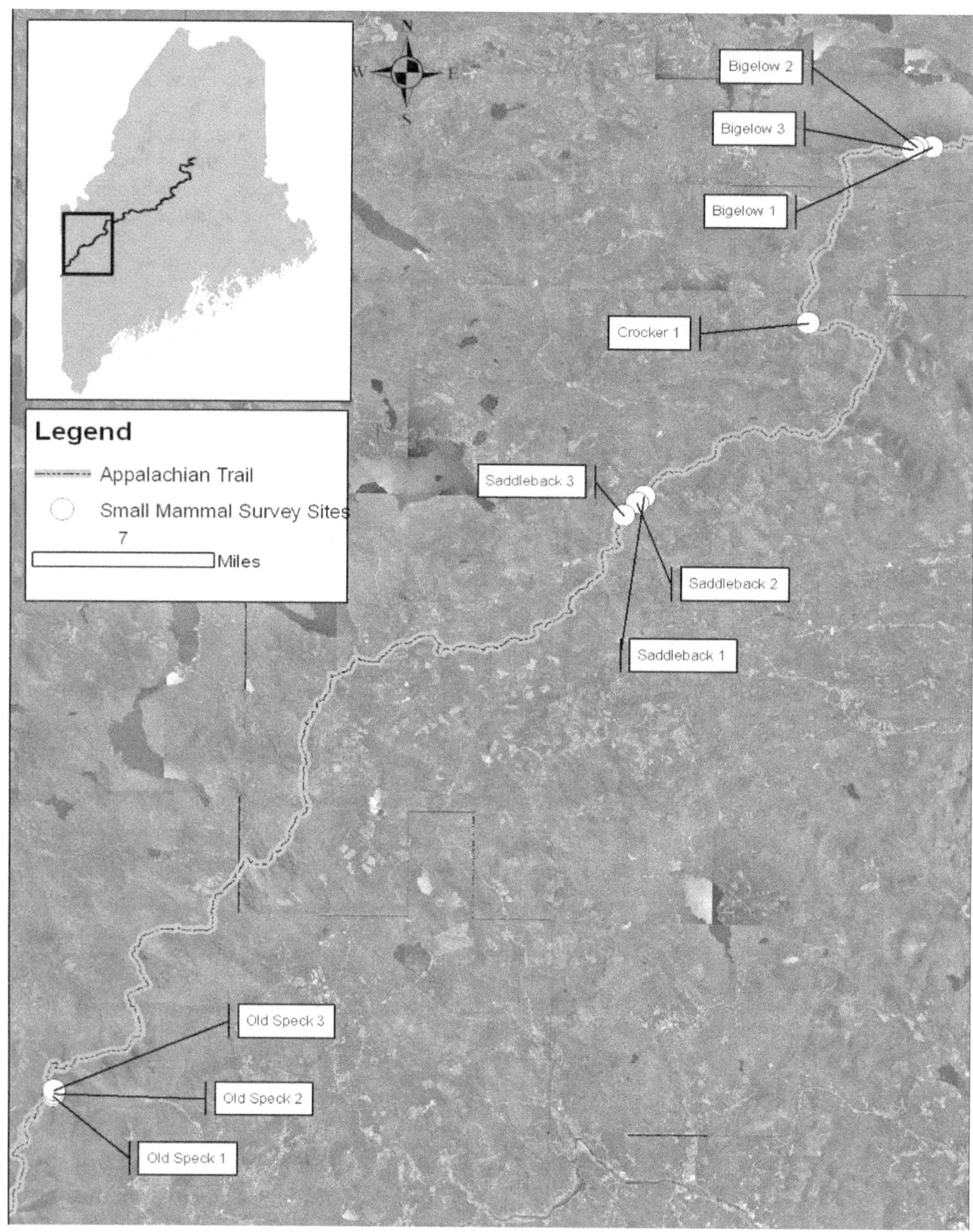

Figure 1. Location of small mammal survey sites along the A.T., Maine in 2006.

Methods

We trapped an average of three nights at each study site and set a total of 80-200 Sherman live-traps, depending on the extent of suitable habitat. Traps were baited with a mixture of oats and peanut butter. They were placed as deeply into a rock or root crevice as possible. A string attached to the trap was tied to a nearby root so the trap could be recovered if it was dragged out of reach into the hole. Most trap lines were non-linear along an elevation gradient through patches of suitable cover. We checked traps the following morning, then traps were re-set and baited as necessary and checked again 24 hours later. The latter procedure was followed for the second trap night as well. If a trap was lost, a replacement trap was set, and the previous night was not counted as a trap-night. Thus, when 110 traps were set for three nights, fewer than 330 trap-nights may have been tallied due to lost traps.

We recorded the number captures per trap at each site. Specimens of target species (northern bog lemming, yellow-nosed vole, long-tailed shrew, or Gaspé shrew) and individuals that could not be identified in the field were collected and frozen (to be later identified and archived), while other identified species were photographed and released unharmed. We pinpointed locations with GPS receivers and described predominant microhabitat features at target species collection sites.

Figure 2. Example of trap placement along the A.T., Maine in 2006.

Results

Overall, the sampling effort totaled 2,997 trap-nights among the 10 survey sites, ranging from 80-200 traps per site and averaging 300 trap-nights per site. We detected target species at two of the 10 sites. Two yellow-nosed voles each were captured at the Crocker and Bigelow Mountain study sites, for a total of four yellow-nosed vole specimens (Table 1). Both of the sites where yellow-nosed voles were collected consisted of steep slopes with some boulders and extensive ledge. The most common small mammal caught during the study was the red-backed vole (*Clethrionomys gapperi*), followed by the masked shrew (*Sorex cinereus*) (Table 2). We only captured one southern bog lemming (*Synaptomys cooperi*) and one meadow vole (*Microtus pennsylvanicus*) during the inventory. Other species found during the study were the woodland jumping mouse (*Napaeozapus insignis*) and deer mouse (*Peromyscus maniculatus*). One of the rock voles and a deer mouse specimen were skinned, stuffed and sent to Acadia National Park for storage.

Table 1. Small mammal sites surveyed along the A.T., Maine in 2006.

Site	Dates	Township	# Target Species	Latitude	Longitude
Saddleback 1	9/19/06 – 9/20/06	Sandy River Plt.	0	44.9362	-70.5044
Saddleback 2	9/19/06 – 9/20/06	Sandy River Plt.	0	44.9323	-70.5096
Saddleback 3	9/19/06 – 9/20/06	Sandy River Plt.	0	44.9245	-70.5196
Bigelow 1	9/22/06 – 9/24/06	Dead River Twp	0	45.1465	-70.2830
Bigelow 2	9/22/06 – 9/24/06	Dead River Twp	0	45.1466	-70.2950
Bigelow 3	9/22/06 – 9/24/06	Dead River Twp	1	45.1452	-70.2986
Old Speck 1	9/27/06 – 9/29/06	Grafton Twp	0	44.5721	-70.9600
Old Speck 2	9/27/06 – 9/29/06	Grafton Twp	0	44.5736	-70.9595
Old Speck 3	9/27/06 – 9/29/06	Grafton Twp	0	44.5757	-70.9594
Crocker 1	10/1/06 – 10/3/06	Carrabasset Valley	1	45.0412	-70.3781

Table 2. Summary of small mammal species captured during trapping surveys along the A.T., Maine in 2006.

Site	Trap Nights	RBVO[1]	MASH	WJMO	DEMO	SOBL	MEVO	YNVO
Saddleback 1	160	1	5	0	2	0	0	0
Saddleback 2	218	3	3	0	0	0	1	0
Saddleback 3	220	1	2	2	1	0	0	0
Bigelow 1	240	2	3	0	1	1	0	0
Bigelow 2	329	12	2	0	0	0	0	0
Bigelow 3	330	9	1	0	0	0	0	2
Old Speck 1	300	7	7	0	1	0	0	0
Old Speck 2	300	7	0	0	0	0	0	0
Old Speck 3	300	11	1	0	1	0	0	0
Crocker 1[2]	600	21	0	0	1	0	0	2
Total	2,997	74	24	2	7	1	1	4

[1] Species Code: RBVO = red-backed vole; DEMO = deer mouse; WJMO = woodland jumping mouse; MASH = masked shrew; SOBL = southern bog lemming; MEVO = meadow vole, YNVO=yellow-nosed vole

[2] One rock vole (APPA 266) and one deer mouse (APPA 266) were collected at the Crocker Mountain site (catalog numbers in parentheses). The study skins were sent to Acadia National Park for long term storage.

Discussion

All of the yellow-nosed voles were found in the southwestern region of the study area. The two mountains where this species was collected are in Maine's western mountains (e.g. Bigelow Mountain Range), which are all above 2,500 feet in elevation, and are steeply sloped and rocky. The two collection sites were also dominated by hardwood forests, and loosely matched the microhabitat characteristics described by Beuch et al. (1977) as sparse overstory with sparse herbaceous cover.

We did not capture any northern bog lemmings despite specifically targeting sites with the appropriate habitat for this species of special concern. Conversely, the MEDIF&W did find northern bog lemmings when they trapped sites along the A.T. in the western mountains (Hermann et al. 2003). However, the latter study used snap-traps instead of the live-capture Sherman traps that were used for the current study (the permit that authorized this project prohibited snap-traps). This is an important point as the two methods can have quite different results. In fact, authors of previous studies have noted the ineffectiveness of live-traps for capturing Northern bog lemmings (Reichel and Beckstrom 1994). They mention that the use of Sherman live-traps: 1) is labor intensive throughout the trapping period; 2) has very low success with any bait tried; and 3) results in at least some mortality (four of six known captures). Instead, snap-trapping for bog lemmings is much more successful and appears to be the method of choice for initial survey work to find new populations, both from an economic and time-constraint view. Therefore, we do not recommend making any conclusions as to the presence/absence of northern bog lemmings at our 2006 study sites. Future efforts to document northern bog lemming range along the A.T. should use the most effective trapping methods.

Although not a target species in this study, the single meadow vole captured at Saddleback Mountain is noteworthy. This species is broadly distributed, but uncommon in the extensively high elevation wooded tracts that are prevalent in western Maine. Meadow voles are occasionally found in such unlikely places and potentially represent a strong competitor for the more "range-limited" small mammals targeted in this study (Mass. Wildlife, T. French, pers. comm.). The presence of a meadow vole in this location may be due to the presence of a ski area where the trails form a corridor of suitable habitat leading from lower elevations to high elevations where this specimen was trapped.

If a target species was present but we failed to detect it, several explanations are possible. Rodent populations, in general, go through cycles of low and high population numbers. Therefore, it is possible that populations of northern bog lemmings, for example, were lower than in previous years when they were detected. Also, as mentioned above our trapping methods may have limited our ability to detect these rare species, and we could have under-sampled some sites. Also, given the species' rare status, it is also plausible that we were simply "unlucky" in detecting some species, especially at sites particularly suited for the target species. We recommend further study of these species' distribution along the A.T.

Bat Survey

Introduction
There are over 1,000 known species of bats in the world. Forty-six species of bats reside in North America, eight of which occur in Maine. Bats in the northeastern United States range in size from the tiny eastern small-footed bat (*Myotis leibii*; three to four grams) to the hoary bat (*Lasiurus cinereus*; 25 grams). Bats are a cryptic species and can be extremely difficult to study. Because of factors that relate to the bats' natural history and vulnerability to anthropogenic stressors, over half of the species in the United States are listed as endangered or threatened, or are under consideration for listing.

Little Brown Bat
The little brown bat (*Myotis lucifugus*) is abundant throughout forested areas of the U.S. as far north as Alaska. This species is commonly associated with humans, often forming nursery colonies containing hundreds, sometimes thousands, of individuals in buildings, attics, and other man-made structures (Barbour and Davis 1969).

Northern Long-eared Bat
The northern long-eared bat (*Myotis septentrionalis*) is widely distributed across eastern North America from Manitoba across southern Canada to Newfoundland, south to northern Florida, west through the south central states and northwest to the Dakotas. It is found in dense forest stands and chooses maternity roosts beneath exfoliating bark and in tree cavities, much like the Indiana Bat (*Myotis sodalis*). The northern long-eared bat also relies upon caves and underground mines for hibernation sites, where it typically chooses cooler sites than other *Myotis* species (Barbour and Davis 1969).

Big Brown Bat
The big brown bat *(Eptesicus fuscus)* is found in virtually every American habitat ranging from timberline meadows to lowland deserts. It is often abundant in suburban areas of mixed agricultural use and is most abundant in deciduous forest areas (Barbour and Davis 1969). This species ranges from extreme northern Canada, throughout the United States and south to the extreme southern tip of Mexico. Typically, these bats form maternity colonies beneath loose bark and in small cavities of pine, oak, beech, bald cypress and other trees. Common maternity roosts today can be found in buildings, barns, bridges, and even bat houses. Small beetles are their most frequent prey, yet big brown bats will consume prodigious quantities of a wide variety of night-flying insects (Barbour and Davis 1969).

Silver-haired Bat
Silver-haired bats (*Lasionycteris noctivagans*, Figure 3) are among the most common bats in forested areas of America, most closely associated with coniferous or mixed coniferous and deciduous forest types, especially in areas of old growth (Barbour and Davis 1969). They form maternity colonies almost exclusively in tree cavities or small hollows. Like many forest-roosting bats, silver-haired bats will switch roosts throughout the maternity season. Because silver-haired bats are dependent upon roosts in old growth areas, managing forests for diverse age structure and maintaining forested corridors are important to these bats (Barbour and Davis 1969).

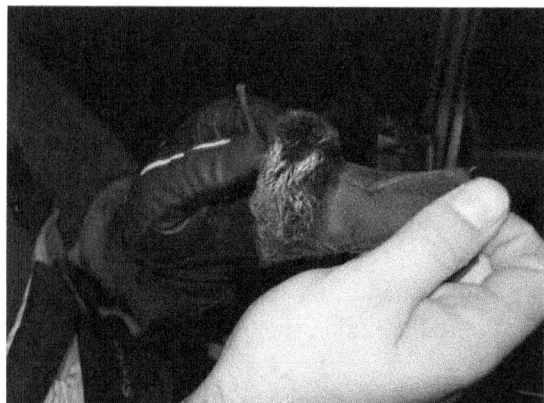

Figure 3. Silver-haired bat captured at Bear River along the A.T., Maine in 2006.

Eastern Red Bat

Eastern red bats (*Lasiurus borealis*) are North America's most abundant "tree bats" (Figure 4). They are found wherever there are trees east of the Rocky Mountains from Canada to as far south as central Florida. Eastern red bats roost in the foliage of deciduous or sometimes evergreen trees. Despite their bright red color, these bats are rather inconspicuous, looking like dead leaves or pinecones. They are perfectly camouflaged as they hang curled up in their furry tail membranes, suspended from a single foot, twisting slightly in the breeze. For the most part, red bats are solitary, coming together only to mate and to migrate. Females even roost singly when rearing young. Unlike most bats, eastern red bats often give birth to twins and can have litters of up to five young, though three young is the average (Barbour and Davis 1969).

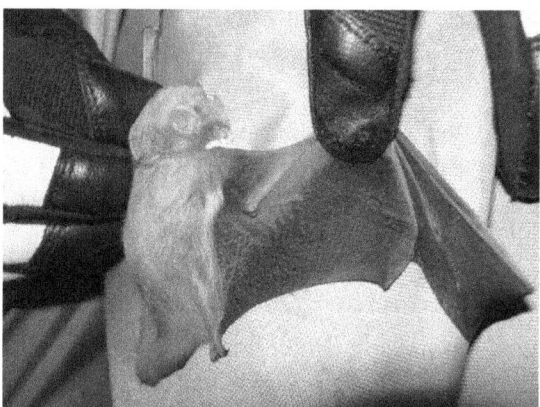

Figure 4. A red bat captured at Crocker Cirque along the A.T., Maine in 2006.

Hoary Bat

Hoary bats (*Lasiurus cinereus*, Figure 5) are one of America's largest bats. With their long, dense, white-tipped fur, they have a frosted, or hoary, appearance. Humans rarely get the chance to see these bats; they are not attracted to houses or other human structures, and stay well hidden in foliage throughout the day. They typically roost 10-15 feet up in trees along forest borders. In summer, hoary bats don't emerge to feed until after dark, but during migration they may be seen soon after sundown. They sometimes make round trips of up to 24 miles on the first foraging flight of the night, and then make several shorter trips, returning to the day roost about an hour before sunrise. Between late summer and early fall, they start their long journey south, migrating to subtropical and possibly even tropical areas to spend the winter (Barbour and Davis 1969).

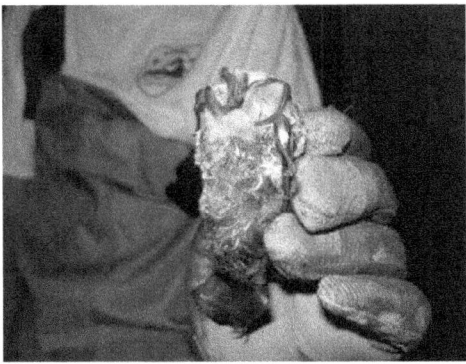

Figure 5. A hoary bat captured at Stratton Brook along the A.T., Maine, 2006.

Eastern Small-footed Bat

The eastern small-footed bat (*Myotis leibii*) is a Species of Special Concern in Maine. Its habits are not well known, making it difficult to optimize survey techniques. Only five small-footed bats have ever been found in Maine, two of which were in hibernacula (MEDIF&W, K. Morris, pers. comm.), indicating that this species is relatively rare. It is a species that does not reach the far north latitudes and just how far north it can occur in Maine is unknown. This survey was designed to capture or acoustically detect small-footed bats and other bat species along the Appalachian National Scenic Trail (A.T.) of Maine.

Study Area

The seven bat study sites (Figure 6) were determined based upon previous knowledge of species distributions (MEDIF&W, Karen Morris, pers. comm.) and species habitat preferences, as well as accessibility. We used USGS topographic maps, ground and aerial surveys of the study area to determine bat inventory locations along the A.T. corridor. We largely focused on rocky talus slopes where bats tend to day roost. Our target Species of Special Concern, the eastern small-footed bat, has a limited distribution in Maine. However, there had been previous observations of small-footed bats in Carrabassett Valley Township near the A.T. in hibernacula. Therefore, we strategically selected a study site in this Township.

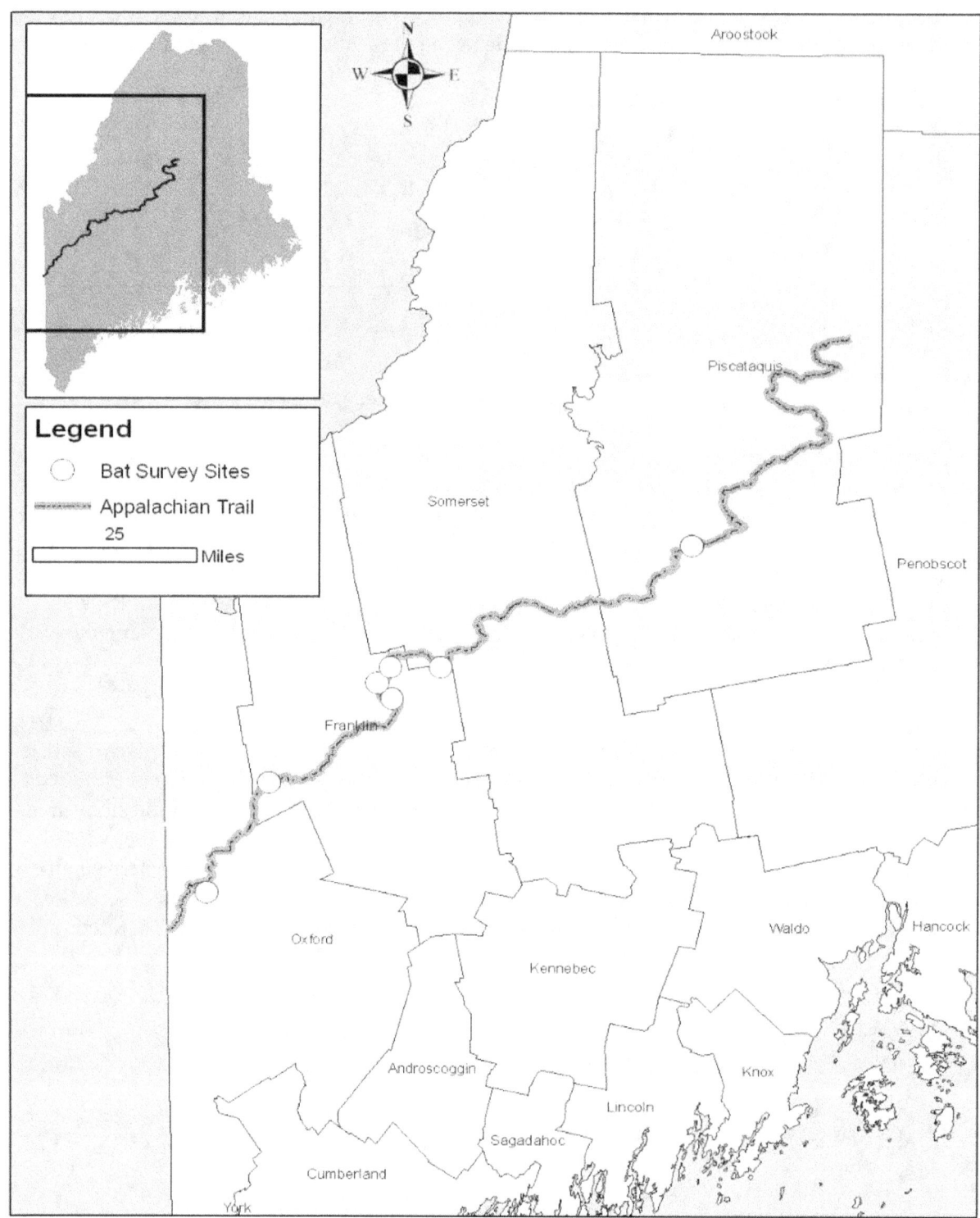

Figure 6. Location of bat study sites along the A.T., Maine in 2006.

Methods

Mist nets and Pettersson ultrasonic detection equipment were used at all seven sites starting in late June and continuing through late July and early August of 2006. One to three single-high (3 meters) mist nets, and one or two triple-high (12 meters) mist nets, were set up for 1-3 nights at each site. Due to tree canopy, road width, and logistics not all nets were put up at each site; for some sites triple high nets were too tall and other sites single nets were too small. Nets were strung between trees along small logging roads, streams, and rivers in such a way that the bats were forced to fly through the net if they were using the corridor. Nets were left in place for consecutive nights (Figure 7). Roads were chosen that led towards water, under the assumption that bats would fly towards the water to drink and feed after leaving their daytime roosts. Mature trees or ledges that would provide good roosting habitat also surrounded the roads. Nets were set at dusk and monitored until at least 2300 h and if bats were being captured, nets were left up until as late as 0100 h. All bats captured were identified to species, basic biometric measurements were recorded and reproductive status was checked (Appendix). Photographs were taken and bats were then released unharmed.

Figure 7. Example of mist net set-up along the A.T., Maine in 2006.

A Pettersson ultrasonic bat detector was deployed for approximately 2 hours during each night we mist netted. The detector was situated away from the nets so people checking them would not contribute false recordings. Bat calls were recorded and examined to determine species that were feeding in the area. The Sonobat® call library is sensitive to regional dialects; therefore we expanded our bat call library for Maine. If bats were being detected but not captured, or if an area was not acting as a good funnel or pinch point for capture, we changed net configuration the next night to improve capture probability.

For each bat captured we recorded the following (see Appendix):

> - Time of capture
> - Species
> - Sex and Age
> - Reproductive Status
> - Forearm (mm)
> - Weight (g)

Results

We captured multiple bat species at each of our seven survey locations (Table 3; Figures 8-10). No small-footed bats were captured during the survey; of the six species that were caught or detected with the acoustic monitoring equipment, the most common were northern long-eared bats and little brown bats (Tables 4 and 5). The other species detected with mist nets were the red bat, hoary bat, silver-haired bat, and big brown bat. The highest number of bats captured at a site was 20 at the Barren Cliffs, followed by Rangeley (19) and Crocker Cirque (14).

Table 3. Sites surveyed for bats along the A.T., Maine in 2006.

Site	Date	Equipment Used	Township	Latitude	Longitude
Stratton Brook	6/23/2006 6/24/2006 6/27/2006	Three 8' nets Two 30' nets Pettersson	Wyman Twp	45.11291	-70.35135
Bear River	7/24/2006 7/25/2006 7/26/2006	Three 30' nets[1] Pettersson	Grafton Twp	44.57216	-70.90553
Rangeley	7/30/2006	Two 30' nets Pettersson	Township D	44.63451	-70.56743
Carriage Road	7/31/2006	One 8' net One 30' net Pettersson	Carrabasset Valley	45.11448	-70.19077
Stony Brook Road	8/1/2006	One 8' net One 30' net Pettersson	Carrabasset Valley	45.07544	-70.39205
Barren Cliffs	8/3/2006 8/4/2006	One 8' net* Two 30' nets Pettersson	Elliotsville Twp	45.4086	-69.4157
Crocker Cirque	8/5/2006 8/7/2006	Two 30' nets Pettersson	Carrabasset Valley	45.03942	-70.3446

[1] Indicates maximum netting used on single survey when net sets were variable between survey nights

Table 4. Summary of bat species captured along the A.T., Maine in 2006.

Location	r[1]	EPFU[2]	LABO	LACI	LANO	MYLU	MYSE	Total
Crocker Cirque	3	0	1	0	0	11	2	14
Carriage Rd.	2	0	0	0	0	4	1	5
Stony Brook Rd.	1	0	0	0	0	1	0	1
Rangeley	3	3	0	0	0	6	10	19
Stratton Brook	3	1	0	1	0	0	5	7
Bear River	3	0	0	0	2	1	2	5
Barren Cliffs	3	1	0	0	0	16	3	20
Total	6	5	1	1	2	39	23	71

[1] r = species richness
[2] Species Codes: EPFU=big brown bat, LABO=red bat, LACI=hoary bat, LANO=silver-haired bat, MYLU=little brown bat, MYSE=northern long-eared bat

Table 5. Summary of bat calls by species detected along the A.T., Maine in 2006.

Location	r[1]	Myotis sp.[2]	LACI[2]	LABO[2]	LANO[2]	EPFU[2]	Total
Stratton Brook	3	6	1	0	0	2	9
Bear River	2	11	0	0	6	0	17
Rangeley	3	36	1	0	0	2	39
Carriage Road	4	7	1	2	0	2	12
Crocker Cirque	3	10	0	2	0	1	13
Stony Brook Rd	1	8	0	0	0	0	8
Barren Cliffs	2	16	0	0	0	3	19
Total	10	94	3	4	6	10	117

[1] r = species richness
[2] Species Codes: EPFU=Big Brown, LABO=Red, LACI=Hoary, LANO=Silver-haired, Myotis sp.= any Myotis species

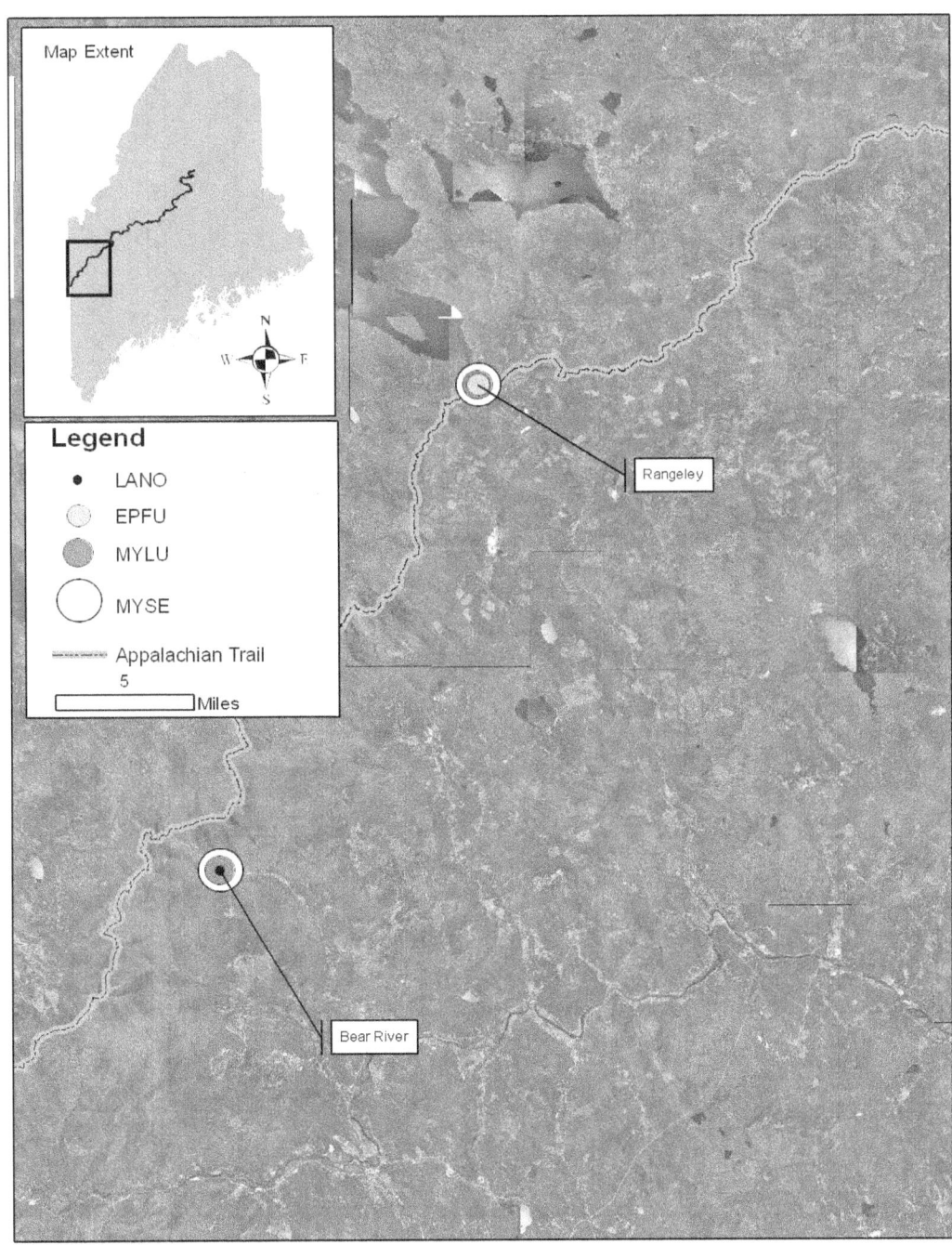

Figure 8. Species of bats captured at Rangeley and Bear River survey sites along the A.T., Maine in 2006.

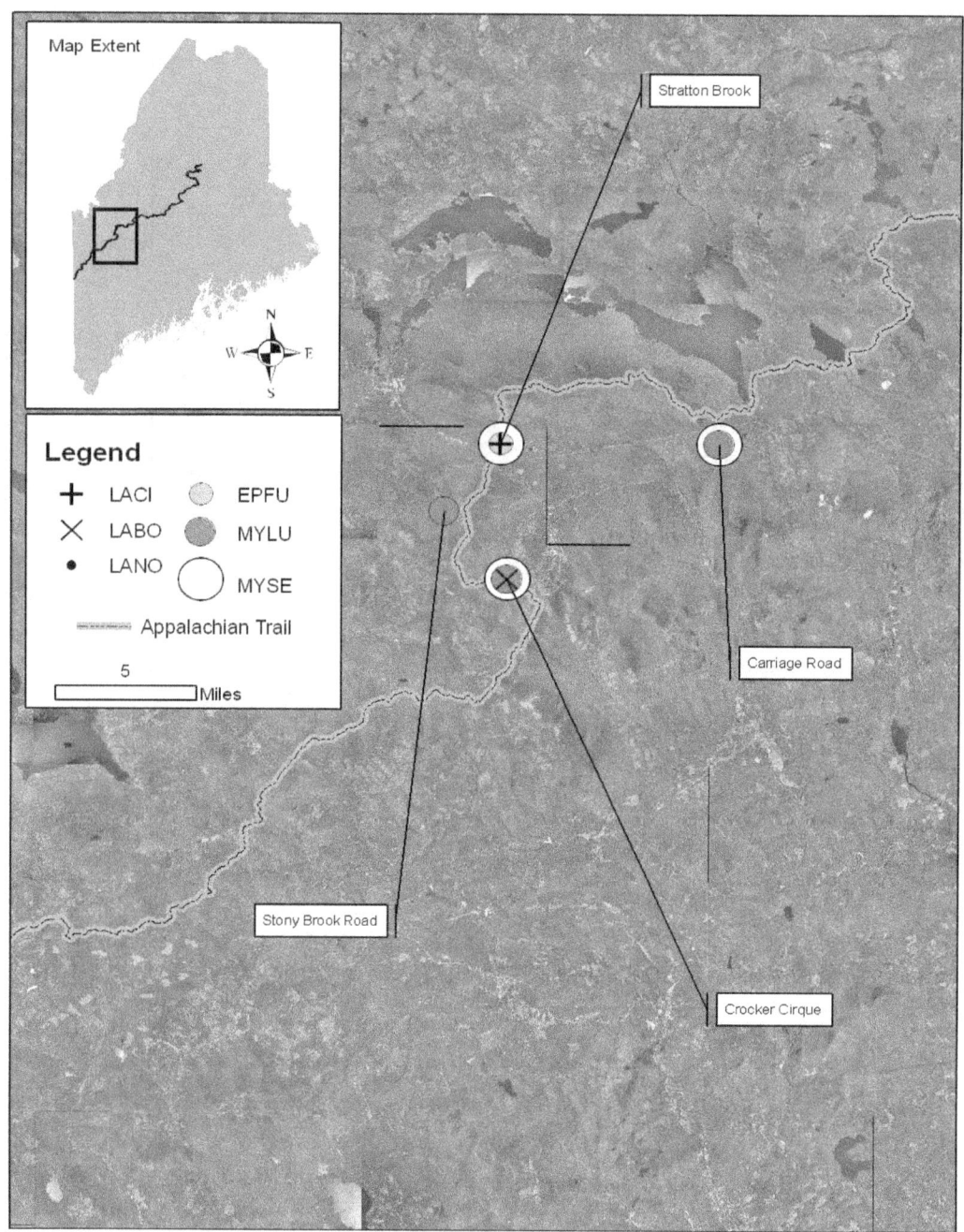

Figure 9. Species of bats captured at the Stratton Brook, Carriage Rd, Crocker Cirque, and Stony Brook Road survey sites along the A.T., Maine in 2006.

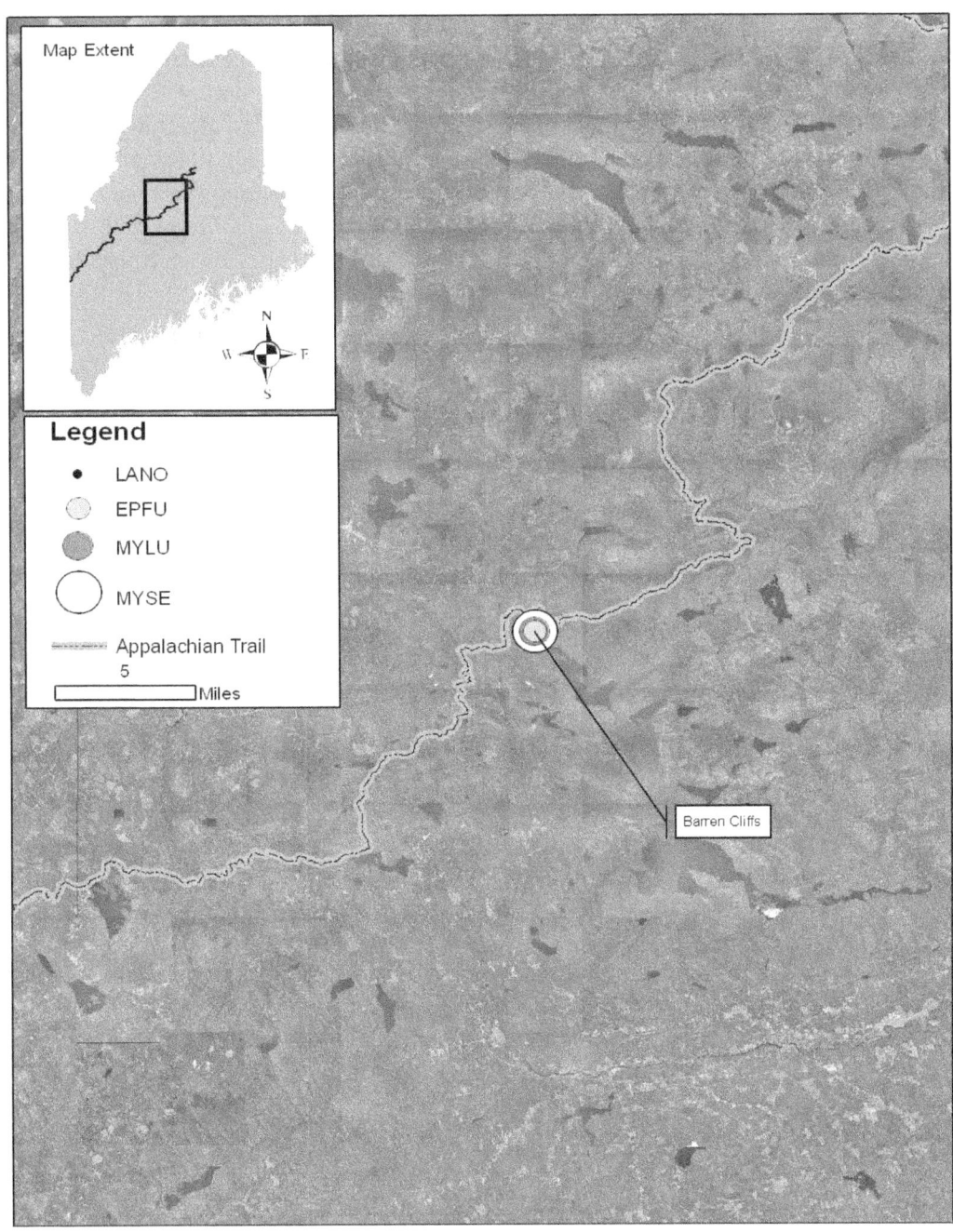

Figure 10. Species of bats captured at the Barren Cliffs survey site along the A.T., Maine in 2006.

Bat calls were recorded and examined using Sonobat® to determine species using the surveyed area to feed. The use of acoustic sampling can increase our detections if, for example, not all bat species were captured by mist nets at a site. The Sonobat® call library is sensitive to regional dialects; therefore we expanded our bat call library for the A.T. area by validating A.T. bat dialects through the "tagging" of each new A.T. bat species. Tagging entailed attaching a string to a bat and allowing it to fly in a specified area to allow a recording of its echolocation calls. New calls were inserted into the Sonobat® call library and used for identifying A.T. bats. It was difficult to differentiate the *Myotis* species of bats using Sonobat®, so all *Myotis* bat calls were lumped together even though this could represent at least three different species (northern long-eared, small-footed, and little brown bats).

Discussion

There has been very little documentation of bat species and bat ecology in Maine. In general, very little is known about the limiting factors for bat species in New England. Through our inventory we were able to document the presence of several bat species of concern along the A.T. in 2006. Some of the special concern species, such as the red bat, hoary bat, and silver-haired bat are noteworthy because of the lack of recent documentation in Maine. Little is known about these species' population sizes, ranges, and habits except that none of these species hibernate in caves. It is believed that these forest dwelling bats are increasingly threatened by the development of wind-power plants throughout their range. Bodies of these species are being recovered in the hundreds to thousands at wind power sites across the northeast (Reynolds 2006), which makes these species of increased interest to biologists. The two silver-haired bats captured are interesting, as this bat species is often associated with old-growth forests, which are almost non-existent in Maine. It is possible that the A.T. corridor is providing an undisturbed habitat, which silver-haired bats prefer, and a migration route for several of these cryptic species of bats. Woodland management practices can and most likely have negatively affected bat populations in Maine. Increasingly, researchers are recognizing the complex habitat needs of bats (Zimmerman and Glanz 2000). Zimmerman and Glanz (2000), when evaluating bat habitat in eastern Maine, noted that the management of bat habitat should be considered at multiple spatial and temporal scales. Bats require a complex mix of habitats, included old-growth wooded forests for roosting, as well as open areas and wetlands for feeding. Therefore, the presence of all such elements should be evaluated when considering bat conservation and bat presence or absence along the A.T. corridor.

The small-footed bat, a species of great conservation concern, both federally and in Maine, was not detected during this survey. The small-footed bat is easily identified in the hand but can be difficult to identify from other *Myotis* spp. using their calls. This species is relatively uncommon in Maine with most of its previous occurrences located in southern portions of Maine (MEDIF&W, K. Morris, pers. comm., Zimmerman and Glanz 2000). However, based on our limited field efforts, failure to capture small-footed bats does not necessarily indicate that the range of this species does not extend along the A.T. There is a historical record of a small-footed bat in Carrabasset Valley, and from other works documenting roosting habitat of this species, it is a possibility that this bat may roost along the A.T. corridor in the Bigelow Mountains (MEDIF&W, K. Morris, pers. comm.). Researchers have noted that the abundance of the eastern small-footed bat is extremely difficult to assess or predict (Erdle and Hobson 2001), and mist netting efforts concentrating on streams or ponds may be ineffective at determining the presence of this species. Alternatively, it is recommended that bat survey guidelines for rocky ridge tops, quarries, cliff faces, and rock wall outcrops and caves be developed and implemented in the future, especially for this uncommon species (Erdle and Hobson 2001). Similar procedures and techniques for small-footed bat inventories should also be developed along the A.T.

Canada Lynx Survey

Introduction

The Canada lynx (*Lynx canadensis*) is both state and federally threatened, and Maine is the only state in the eastern United States with a steady population. Historical records and reproduction data from 1833 to 1999 in northern Maine (including regions along the A.T. corridor) confirm the presence of lynx, as well as observations of lynx kittens (Hoving et al. 2003). Over time, lynx have retreated northward into Maine due to increased human presence, climate change, and changes in forest communities (from coniferous to deciduous) (Hoving et al. 2003). Current models used to predict lynx habitat throughout the northeast predict the presence of populations in north central Maine (Hoving et al. 2005, Carroll, 2007). However, more accurate distribution information is needed in order to facilitate conservation of the lynx in Maine, especially considering the recent efforts of the U.S. Fish and Wildlife Service to designate more than 10,000 square miles of Maine forestland as critical habitat for Canada lynx.

The occurrence and distribution of lynx in Maine depends heavily on habitat availability at several spatial and temporal scales (Hoving et al. 2005), as well as the cyclic population of snowshoe hares (*Lepus americanus*). Lynx will often hunt in stands with a high density of snowshoe hares, but also choose foraging sites based on accessibility, which can be described by stand level characteristics including: conifer sapling density (7,000-11,000 stems/ha); canopy closure < 60% in stands where snowshoe hares occur, as well as the basal area of live trees (18-21 m^2/ha) (Fuller et al. 2007). Lynx consistently selected sites that were undergoing self-thinning, which likely increased the visibility and vulnerability of hares (Fuller et al. 2007), as well as accessibility and movement for lynx. Fuller et al. (2007) suggest that the latter results stress "the importance of an interaction between prey density and prey access in determining lynx foraging success and habitat selection." However, lynx require more than just good foraging habitat; they also need the appropriate habitat for maternal dens. Slough (1999) found that a common feature of lynx maternal dens sites across its range is the preferred use of coarse woody debris most often found in mature forests. Another important "denning" habitat characteristic identified by Slough (1999) is dense horizontal and vertical structure which protects kittens from both mammalian and avian predation. Increasingly, researchers are recognizing the importance of good forest management and large tracts of undeveloped forest lands to lynx populations in Maine. Accordingly, several inventories around the state have been tracking the distribution of lynx in Maine with the goal of conserving both this rare species and delineating its necessary habitat.

One such inventory, conducted by the MEDIF&W, has been surveying subsets of different ecoregions throughout Maine. Each region is surveyed to document the occurrence and distribution of rare species. The Canada Lynx is a target species for these surveys. Due to the effectiveness of snow-tracking surveys for detecting lynx presence in Maine, and based on a methodology designed and tested on a study area with radio collared lynx, it has been selected as the most efficient survey method for documenting lynx occurrence. Surveys have been completed in four ecoregion subsets - Boundary Plateau and St John Uplands (2003), Aroostook Hills and Lowlands (2004), Eastern Lowlands (2006/07) to identify the current distribution of lynx in Maine. We implemented a similar survey, using MEDIF&W's protocol, to determine the presence of Canada Lynx along the Appalachian Trail.

Study Area

We selected nine survey sites, each consisting of one Maine Township (Figures 11-20). Sites were selected based on the suitability of habitat conditions for lynx, previously reported lynx sightings, as well as A.T. proximity. If possible we resurveyed some MEDIF&W sites if they were close to the A.T. Other sites not previously surveyed were chosen based on a predictive model developed by Hoving et al. (2005).

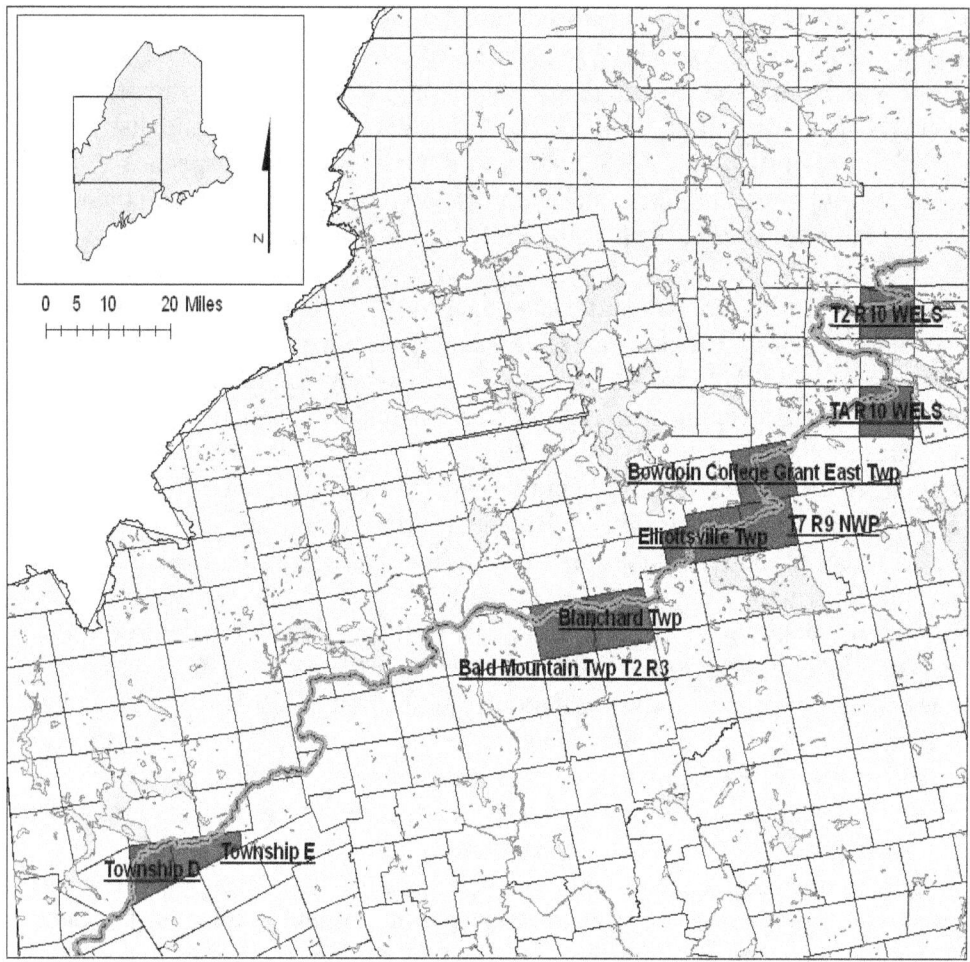

Figure 11. Map of the Maine townships surveyed for lynx in 2007- 08.

24

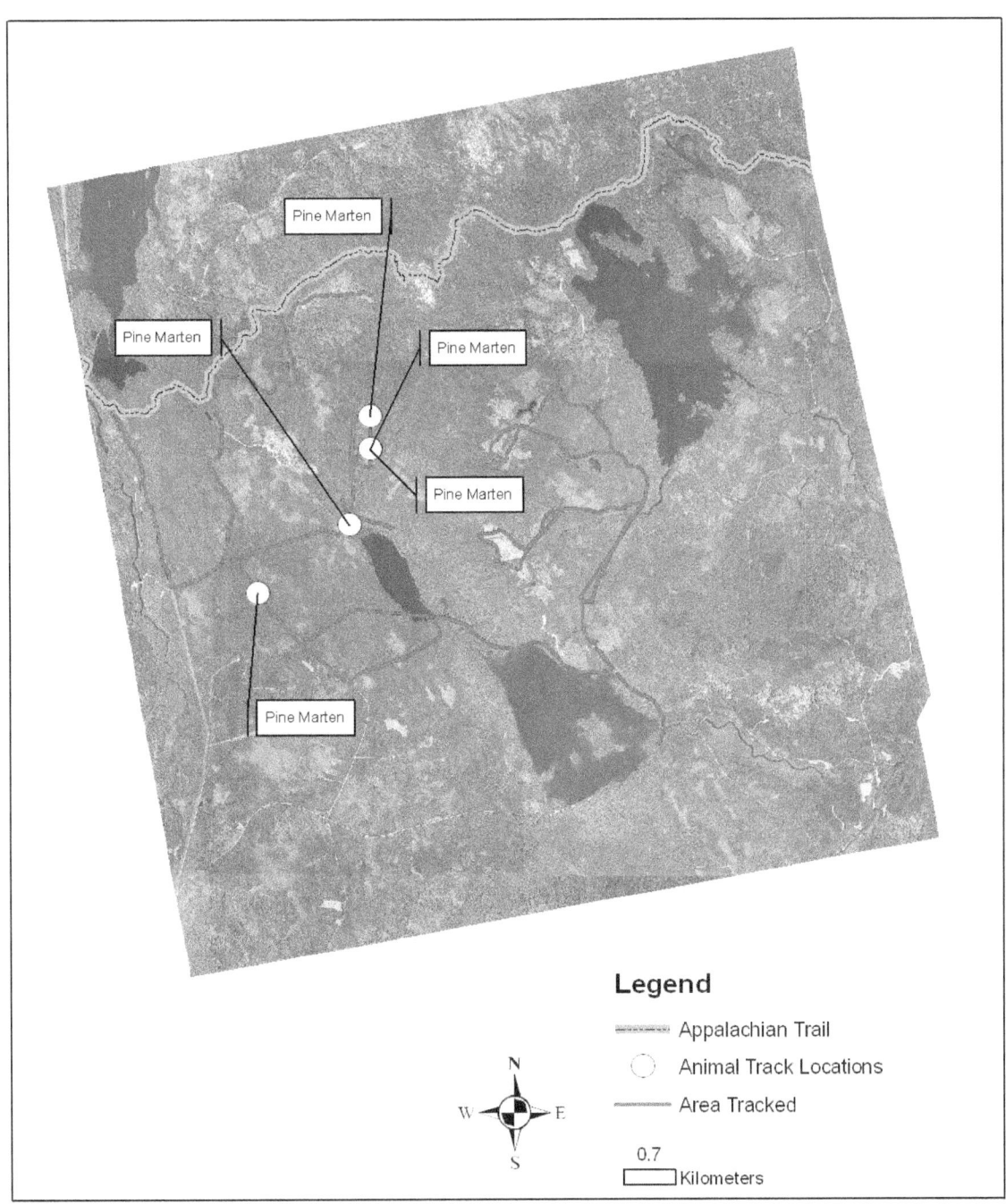

Figure 12. Winter Tracking Survey - Bald Mountain Township, Somerset County, Maine, 2008.

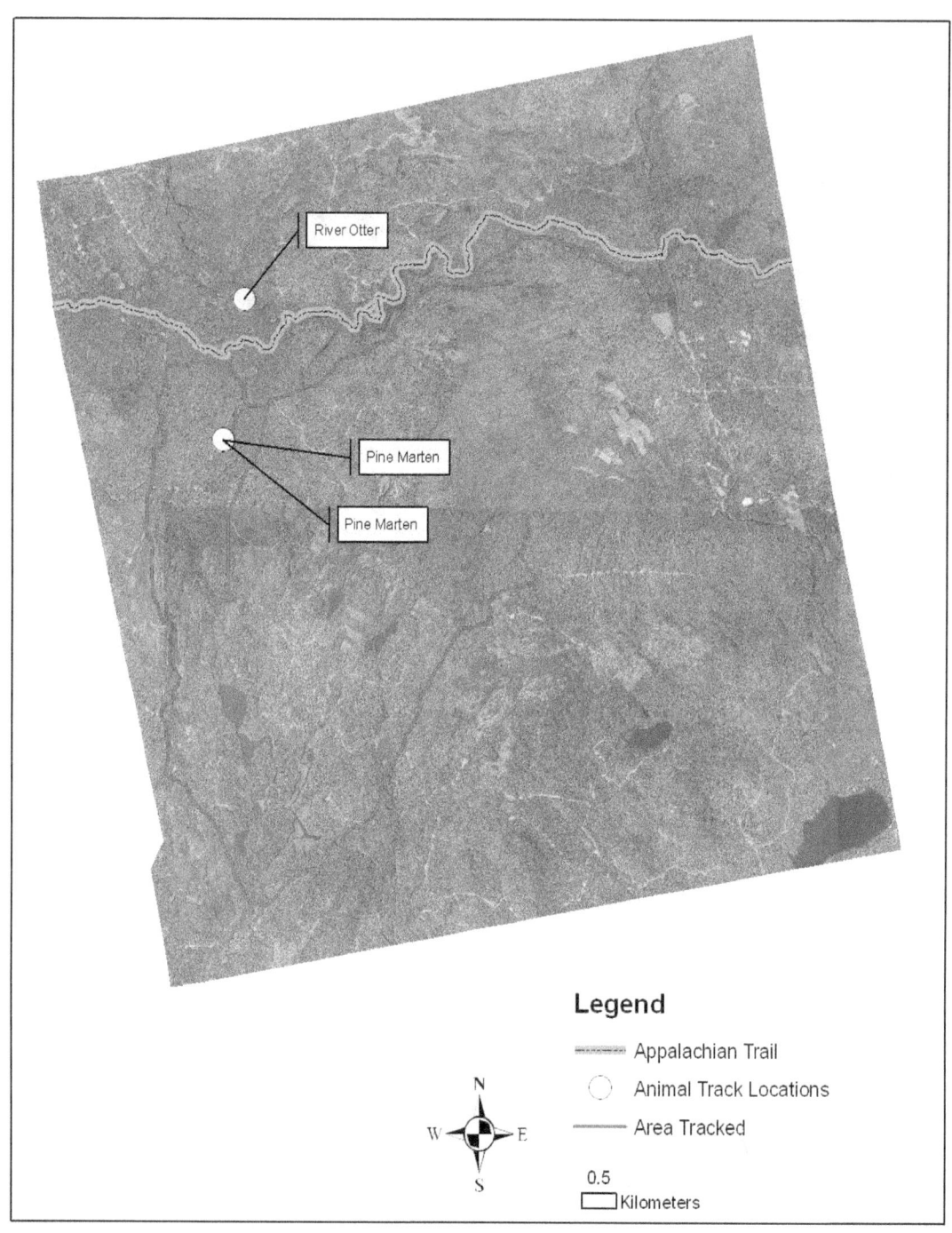

Figure 13. Winter Tracking Survey - Blanchard Township, Piscataquis County, Maine, 2008.

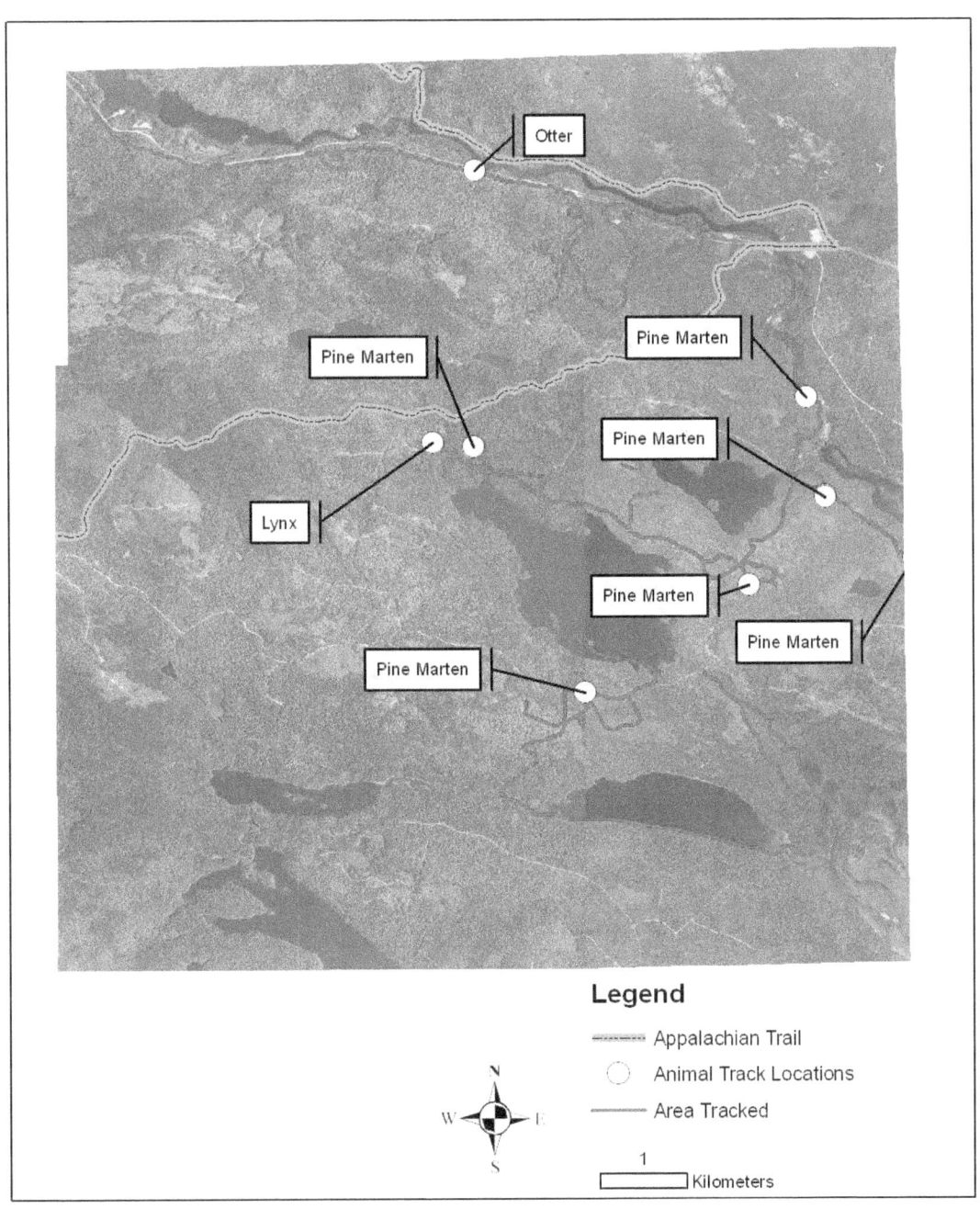

Figure 14. Winter Tracking Survey - T2 R10 WELS Township, Piscataquis County, Maine, 2008.

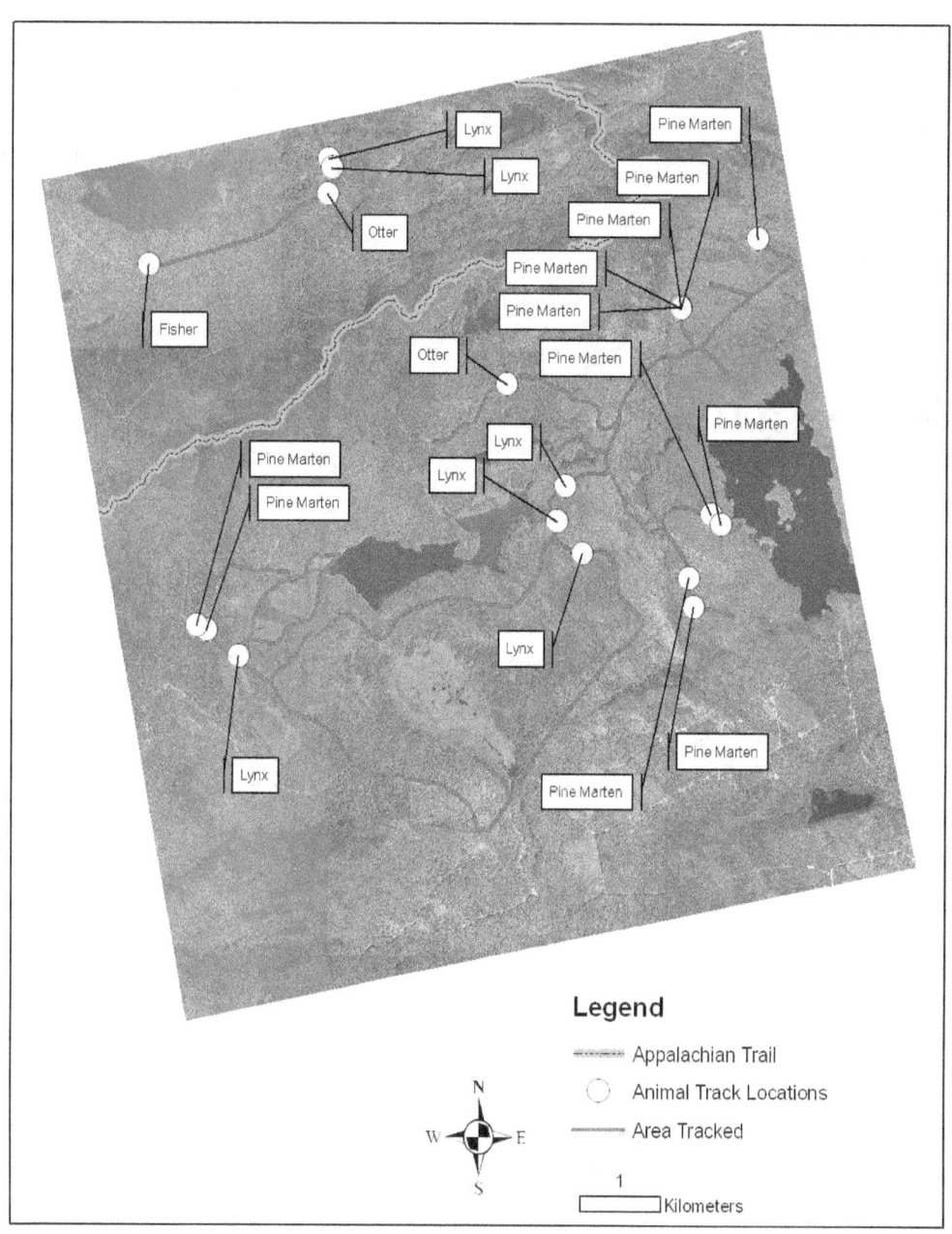

Figure 15. Winter Tracking Survey - T7 R9 NWP Township, Piscataquis County, Maine, 2008.

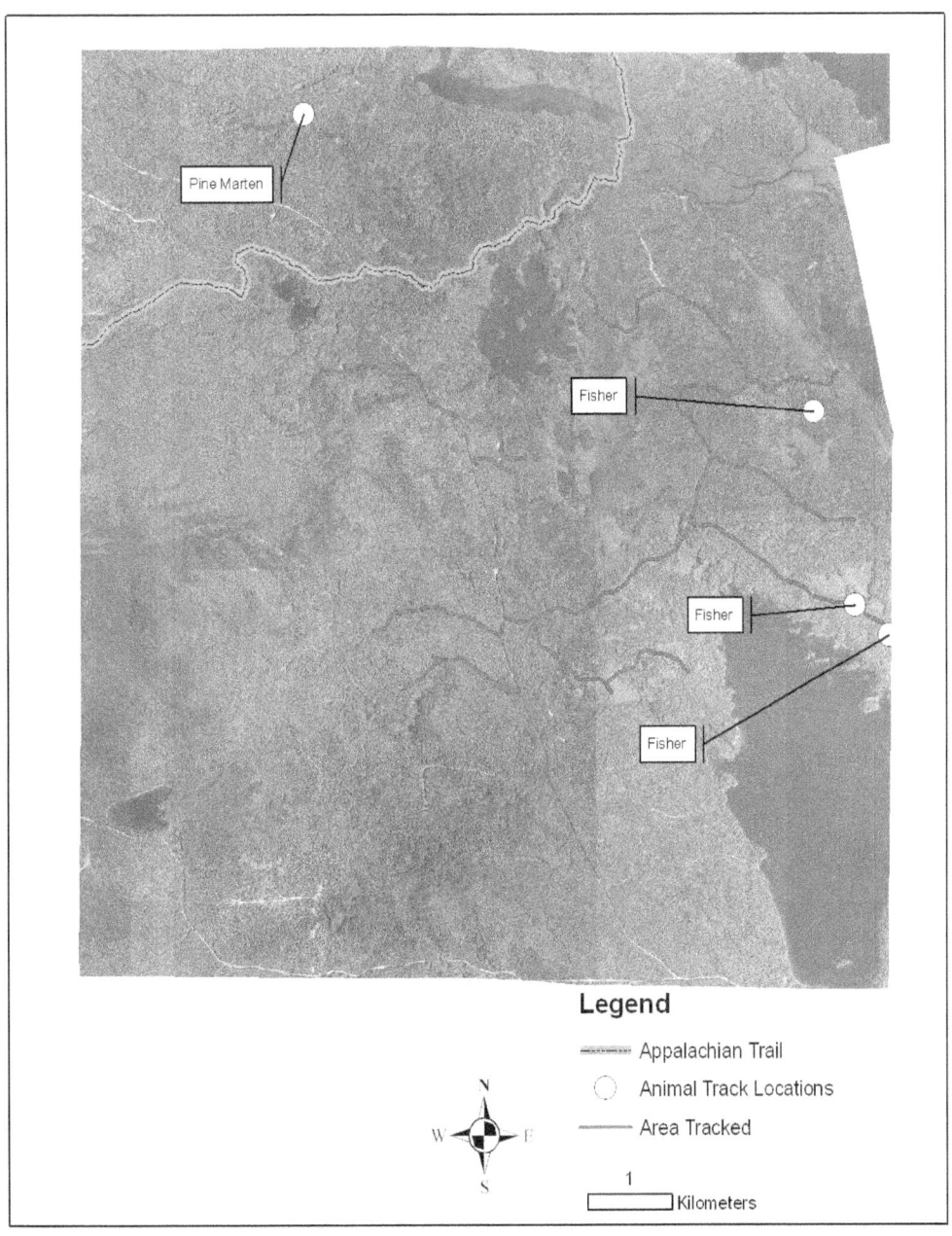

Legend

Appalachian Trail

Animal Track Locations

Area Tracked

N
W E
S

1
Kilometers

Figure 16. Winter Tracking Survey - TA R10 WELS Township, Piscataquis County, Maine, 2008.

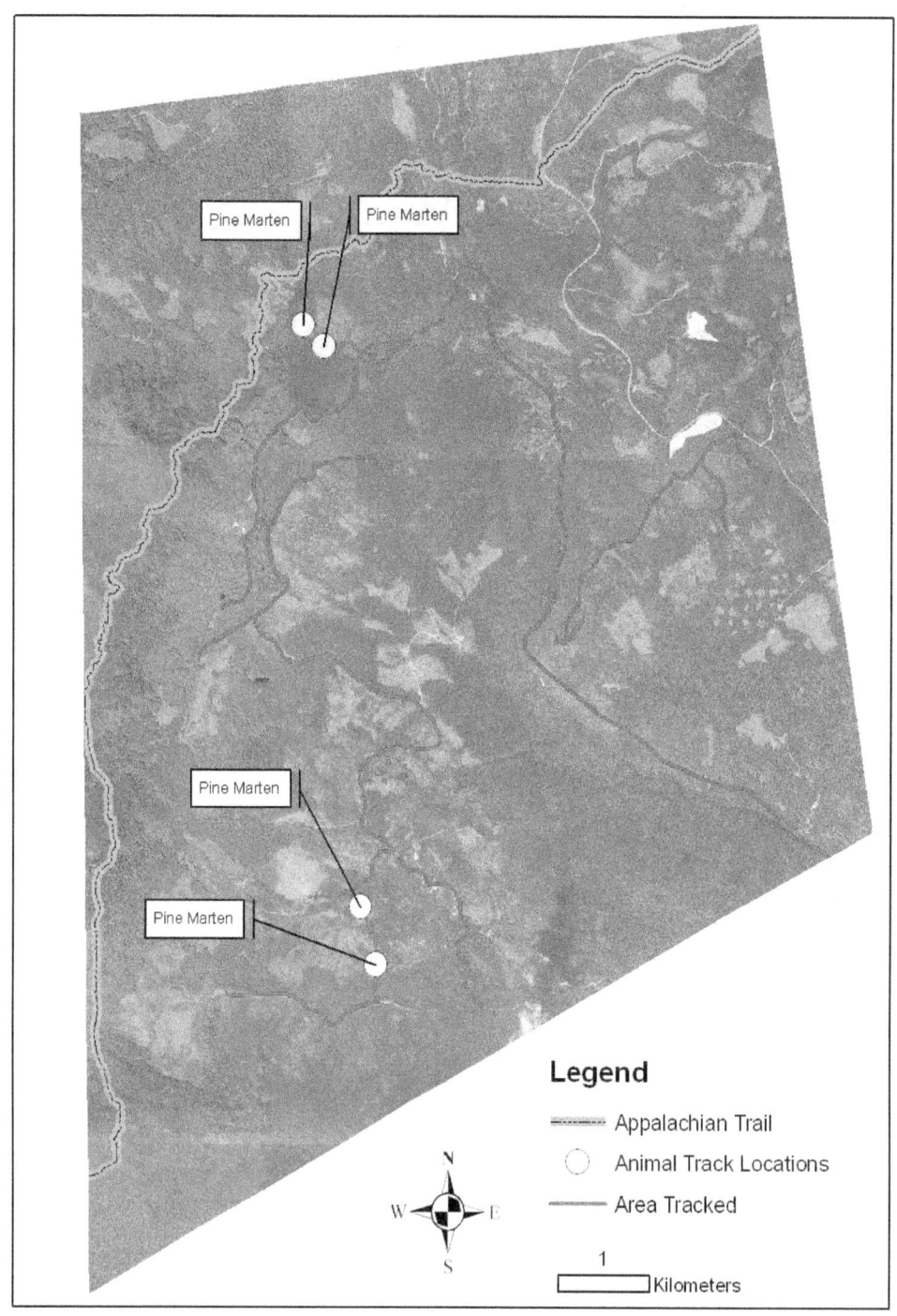

Figure 17. Winter Tracking Survey - Township D, Franklin County, Maine, 2008.

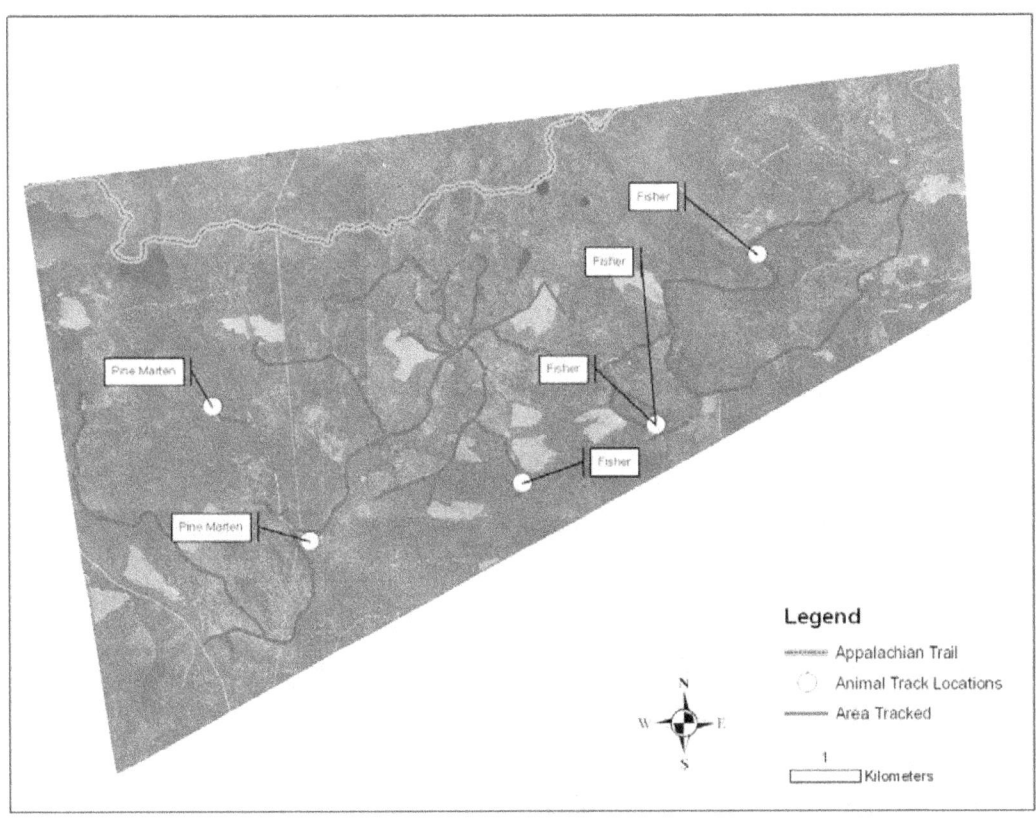

Figure 18. Winter Tracking Survey - Township E, Franklin County, Maine, 2008.

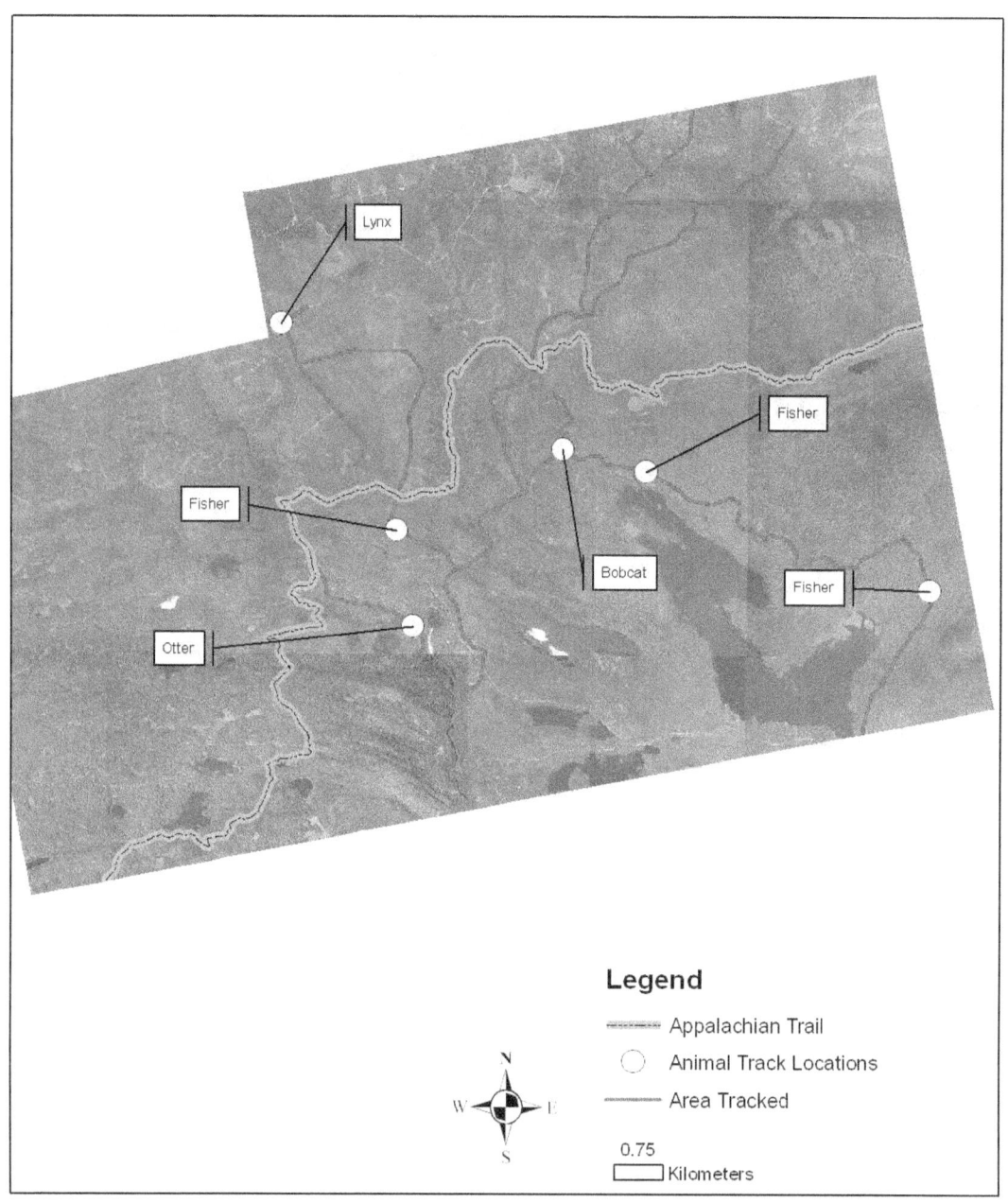

Figure 19. Winter Tracking Survey - Elliotsville Township, Piscataquis County, Maine, 2007.

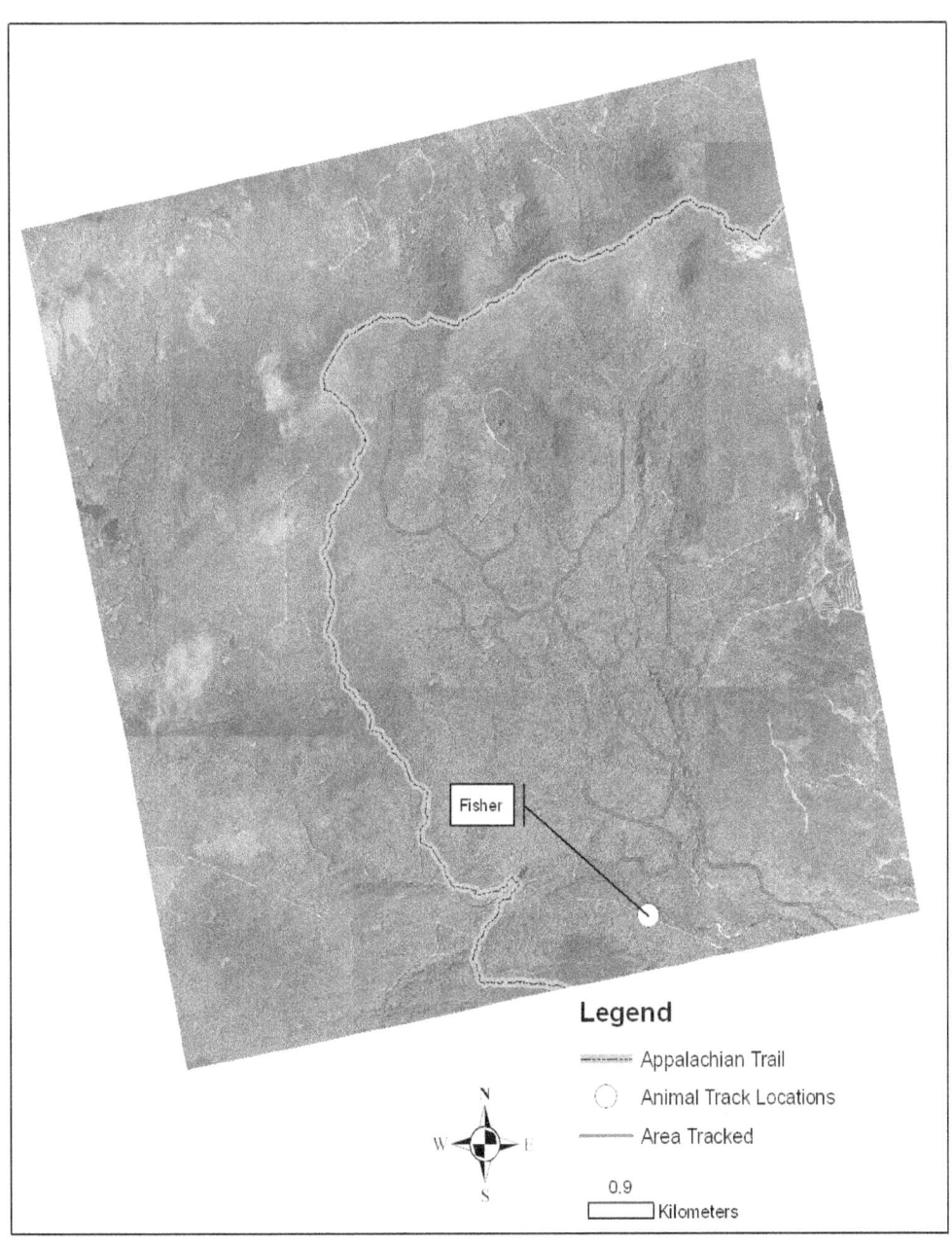

Legend

—————— Appalachian Trail
◯ Animal Track Locations
—————— Area Tracked

N
W ✦ E
S

0.9
Kilometers

Figure 20. Winter Tracking Survey - Bowdoin College Grant East Township, Piscataquis County, Maine, 2007.

Methods

We used snow track surveys to detect lynx presence. Track surveys usually began 24 hours after a snow event, unless winds caused blowing snow to cover tracks. If this was the case, the survey was not started until 24 hours after the wind event ended. This time delay ensured conditions that provided clear track definition, allowed animals time to travel sufficiently following severe weather, and provided a reasonable chance of detecting their presence. Track counts were usually concluded within 24 hours of a snow or wind event, since track identification becomes difficult after 3-4 days. The number of hours after a snow or wind event was recorded in the dataset.

Each township was surveyed once during the winter by two people on snowmobiles, along 55-80 km of roads selected throughout the township. To map our survey routes, a GPS track log was recorded while surveying each township. Track logs were set to establish contact with satellites at a maximum of 30-second intervals to insure that curvature of the road and road distances were adequately recorded. Track logs were always turned off when we re-traveled any survey route (e.g. on dead end roads, we turned the track log off when heading back to our next survey road). Track logs were downloaded onto a PC at the end of each day using the program DNR Garmin (Minnesota Dept. of Natural Resources. 2008).

Predators frequently travel roads and trails, or cross these features several times over a short distance. Following the recommendation of Stephenson and Karczmarczyk (1989), a track intercept was defined as any trail made by a lynx encountered along the survey route that could not be connected to an adjacent lynx trail, based on visual examination from the survey route. When a lynx track was encountered, we recorded the track intercept by obtaining a GPS waypoint where that lynx track crossed the road. We then recorded the coordinates on the datasheet after it had been acquired on the GPS. When a lynx traveled a road, we obtained and recorded a waypoint where it both entered the road and departed the road. At each lynx track intercept, the following additional data were recorded:

Track measurements: For each individual set of tracks, we measured and recorded the track length, track width, stride (toe to toe of the same foot), straddle (measure on outside of tracks), and sinking depth. We took several repeated measurements of different tracks for each of the measurement types and then measurements were averaged.

Direction of travel: Used a compass to determine and record the forward direction of travel.

Number of lynx: Recorded the number of individual lynx (e.g. "solitary individual" or "family group of three").

Track Quality: Recorded the quality of the detected track as follows:

> *Rating 4*: <u>Best</u>; every footprint registered, and detail within prints was very clear. Species identification was essentially absolute based on track details.
>
> *Rating 3*: <u>Good</u>; every print registered, but details were weak, perhaps obscured by snow falling in print. Print details usually visible in microtopographic sites (e.g. tree wells and shadows). Identification based on track details, but gait patterns often needed support.
>
> *Rating 2*: <u>Acceptable</u>; some prints failed to register, and footprint details, if present were visible only in microtopographic sites. Identification based primarily on gait patterns.

Rating 1: <u>Poor</u>; many prints did not register. Track details lacking. Identification was essentially by gait patterns, and may have been possible only in microtopographic sites.

Rating 0: <u>Unacceptable</u>; target species did not leave enough prints to identify gait patterns left.

<u>Photographs</u>: We took several photographs that were close-ups of the track along with several photographs that display the stride and straddle of the track set. A small ruler was included as a scale reference in photographs.

<u>Behavioral data</u>: Recorded behavioral observations (i.e. walking, chasing, and scent marking).

<u>Habitat data</u>: Described the habitat where a lynx track was observed. For example, we noted if the stand was a regenerating or mature forest, noted predominate cover type (S = softwood, H = hardwood, SH = >75% S, HS = >75% H), recorded the height of mature trees (1 = <25 ft, 2=26-45 ft, 3 = 46+ ft) or the height of regeneration. (4 = 1-5 ft, 5 = 6-15 ft, 6 = 16-25 ft), and recorded the density of forest or regeneration. (A = Dense (81-100%), B = Moderate (51-80%), C = Sparse (0-50%)).

Results

Nine townships along the A.T. were surveyed for lynx during the winters of 2007 and 2008 (Table 6; Figures 12-20). Townships were surveyed from January through March over this 2 year period. Eight lynx tracks were detected in three townships: Elliotsville Township, T2R10WELS, and T7R9NWP (Figures 12-20). Several other mammal species were observed during tracking. One of the more common tracks observed were those of pine marten. We observed pine martin tracks in all townships surveyed except Elliotsville, for a total of 32 pine marten detections. Fisher (n = 12) and river otter (n = 5) were the next most abundant species recorded, occurring in five and four of the eight townships, respectively. The least observed species was bobcat with only one individual observed in the Elliotsville Township.

Table 6. Number tracks and species detected by township during snow track surveys along the A.T., Maine in 2007-08.

Township/Species	Survey Date	Bobcat	Fisher	Lynx	Marten	Otter	Total
Bald Mountain (*Fig. 12*)	02/24/2008	0	0	0	5	0	5
Blanchard Twp (*Fig. 13*)	02/17/2008	0	0	0	2	1	3
Bowdoin College Grant East Twp (*Fig. 20*)	02/18/2007	0	1	0	0	0	1
Elliottsville Twp(*Fig. 19*)	03/05/2007	1	3	1	0	1	6
T2R10 WELS (*Fig. 14*)	02/25/2008	0	0	1	7	1	9
T7 R9 NWP (*Fig. 15*)	01/07/2008	0	1	6	11	2	20
TA R10 WELS(*Fig. 16*)	01/05/2008	0	3	0	1	0	4
Township D (*Fig. 17*)	01/25/2008	0	0	0	4	0	4
Township E (*Fig. 18*)	01/17/2008	0	4	0	2	0	6
Total		1	12	8	32	5	58

Discussion

We documented the presence of lynx in three of nine townships, including the northern most township surveyed (T7R9NWP), near Baxter State Park, where they have been observed historically (Hoving et al. 2003), as well as Elliotsville Township, just south of Moosehead Lake, where a population of lynx is known to occur near Lily Bay State Park (MEDIF&W, Jen Vashon, pers. comm.). As mentioned before, the MEDIF&W is currently conducting lynx snow-tracking surveys throughout the several ecoregions of Maine. However, data from those surveys have not yet been made public and the department will survey the western mountains in 2009. Surveys, including this one, will be extremely relevant for determining current and future lynx distributions in Maine and will be key to ensuring that informed decisions are made regarding lynx conservation as well as the designation of critical habitat.

In Maine, the abundance of Canada lynx increases with latitude, mainly due to fewer human settlements and lower use of forestry practices common in the southern parts of the state that reduce and fragment suitable foraging and denning habitat (Poole 2003). Also, at the southern extent of their range snowshoe hare densities may be too low to sustain lynx populations (Bunnell et al. 2006). Snowshoe hare make up over one-third of the diet of Canada lynx (Poole 2003) and their population cycle closely mirrors that of the snowshoe hare. Most lynx populations cycle on an 8-11 year basis, and some of their normal distribution areas may become devoid of lynx for several years during snowshoe hare population lows (Poole 2003). Because of this, it can be assumed that in years of low densities of lynx, in southern portions of their range (e.g. Maine), any additive mortality (e.g. increased trapping pressure) could devastate local populations.

Lynx home range sizes vary among areas, sexes, seasons and cyclical patterns (Poole 2003). In addition, mean home range size in lynx across their range was determined using different methods, making it difficult to compare data from separate studies. Poole (2003) mentions that in southern portions of their range, and during periods of high hare density, home ranges tend to be smaller (13-45 km^2). These ranges can increase 2-10 fold during years of low hare densities, and dispersal distances greater than 500 km have been recorded (Poole 2003). From this, it is reasonable to state that lynx require large tracts of undisturbed habitat, especially during years of low hare densities. Such tracts of suitable habitat are becoming less available as forest practices change, and human habitation of remote areas increases. Human encroachment may also encourage competitor species like coyote and bobcat, which under "normal circumstances" are not sympatric with lynx. Deep snow would ordinarily keep these species separated and limit interspecies competition but the increased number of plowed roads and snowmobile trails further into lynx home ranges may be changing this, and will likely have negative consequences for local lynx populations in Maine. Litvaitis and Harrison (1989) found a negative correlation between bobcat and coyote populations during a period of increasing coyote populations, which they attributed to exploitation competition. When Bunnell et al. (2006) analyzed the potential impacts of coyotes and snowmobiles on lynx conservation in the Intermountain West, they found that the presence of hard-packed trails has the potential to break down the spatial segregation of lynx and coyote populations during annual periods of deep snow. Lynx do have the potential to react to such limiting factors. For example in Cape Breton Island, an isolated population of lynx retreated to higher elevations (Poole 2003). Accordingly, high elevation habitats, like those available along the A.T., may become increasingly important to lynx in Maine.

In conclusion, current and future threats to lynx in Maine are habitat loss and fragmentation due to anthropogenic causes. Increasingly lynx will be required to adapt to increased competition from species that thrive in response to human alteration of habitats, as well as the resultant change of forest communities due to climate change. While lynx may adapt by retreating to higher elevations, it is ultimately the availability of their key prey, snowshoe hare, that determines survival and productivity. How lynx in Maine will respond to these threats is unknown. It will become increasingly important to monitor lynx distributions throughout their range in order to draw conclusions about current and future lynx distributions in Maine. Current snow-tracking efforts throughout the state are considered a highly successful technique used to determine presence of lynx, and we feel confident that our surveys captured a representative distribution of lynx in the townships surveyed. Finally, it will be very important to determine the relative significance of these protected high elevation areas to lynx, to both benefit and influence future decisions regarding lynx conservation in Maine.

Summary of Furbearer Data

Furbearers are those mammals that are harvested primarily for their pelts. In Maine this includes muskrat (*Ondatra zibethicus*), beaver (*Castor canadensis*), mink (*Mustela vison*), otter (*Lontra canadensis*), raccoon (*Procyon lotor*), skunk (*Mephitis mephitis*), red and gray fox (*Vulpes vulpes* and *Urocyon cinereoargenteus* respectively), coyote (*Canis latrans*), marten (*Martes martes*), and fisher (*Martes pennanti*). The harvest of furbearing animals is important both recreationally and economically to many Maine people and contributes significantly to the state's economy. State and federal agencies were tasked with applying science to protect, maintain and restore wildlife populations. The harvest of furbearers became a highly regulated, scientifically monitored activity. Today, as controversy over the use and harvest of furbearers continues, professional wildlife managers find themselves spending considerable time trying to clarify public misconceptions about trapping and furbearer management. The complex issues involved in that management are: habitat loss, animal damage control, public health and safety, and the responsible treatment of animals.

There are many issues involving the conservation and management of furbearers today. Two of the biggest are 1) encroachment and the degradation and destruction of wildlife habitat, and 2) increasing public intolerance of wildlife in populated areas. The continuing loss of wildlife habitat is the most critical issue in wildlife conservation today. Unlike regulated trapping, habitat destruction threatens the existence of wildlife populations and the ecosystems on which they depend. In Maine, the A.T. provides these animals areas of wilderness that is protected and unfragmented by human development. Habitat destruction has eliminated the option to restore some species to areas where they once existed (wolf, mountain lion). Among wildlife scientists, ecologists, and biologists no issue is of greater concern than the conservation of wildlife habitat. Furbearers have economic, ecological, cultural, biological, and aesthetic value. Many people benefit economically from the use of furs and other furbearer products, but can also suffer economic loss from damage or depredation caused by furbearers. Some furbearers (e.g. beaver and muskrat) alter habitat, often to the benefit of many other wildlife species. Furbearers also can help us better understand human health problems, such as effects of environmental pollutants.

Statewide harvest totals were obtained from Fur Dealer Report Booklets (MEDIF&W 2007) and are calculated each year by county and physiographic region. This data enables biologists to estimate the worth of the furbearer resource and, in conjunction with other biological data, helps to objectively manage these species. We used data from the Fur Dealer Report Booklet, required by the state for all pelt sales, to determine the figures listed in Table 7. Fur buyers are required to record all pelt sales in Fur Dealer Report Booklets and trappers were supplied these booklets and instructed to complete and return them within 30 days following the close of the fur-taking season.

The furbearer harvest figures (Table 7) reflect only those furbearers harvested recreationally, (i.e. during the open season) and not those taken outside the open season under nuisance wildlife permits. Fur harvest figures are based on mandatory fur harvest reports which, by state law all trappers (i.e. anyone purchasing a trapping license) must return at the end of the trapping season. It is thought that the fisher and marten have declining populations in Maine. Therefore state agencies have put trapper limits on both species of 25 marten tags and 10 fisher tags per season.

Table 7. Furbearer harvest figures by Maine township summarized from Fur Dealer Report Booklets (2007).

Townships/Species	Beaver	Bobcat	Coyote	Fisher	Grey Fox	Red Fox	Marten	Mink	Otter	Totals
Andover North Surplus	0	0	0	0	0	0	0	0	0	0
Andover West Surplus	1	0	0	0	0	0	0	0	0	1
Bald Mountain Twp.	21	0	1	0	0	1	1	0	1	25
Blanchard Twp.	7	0	0	0	0	0	0	0	0	7
Bowdoin College Grant East	0	0	0	0	0	1	0	0	0	1
Bowtown Twp.	12	0	0	0	0	2	6	0	1	21
Caratunk	12	2	3	1	0	0	6	0	2	26
Carrabassett Valley	2	0	0	1	0	0	4	0	0	7
Carrying Place Town Twp.	0	0	0	0	0	0	0	0	0	0
Carrying Place Twp.	3	0	0	0	0	0	3	0	0	6
Dead River Twp.	0	0	0	0	0	0	5	0	0	5
Elliotsville Twp.	2	0	0	0	0	0	0	0	0	2
Grafton TWP	10	1	2	0	0	0	0	5	2	20
Madrid Twp.	6	1	9	5	0	7	6	0	0	34
Monson	18	0	1	2	0	1	2	0	1	25
Mount Abram Twp.	1	0	0	2	0	3	3	0	0	9
Mt. Katahdin Twp.	0	0	0	0	0	0	0	0	0	0
Rainbow Twp.	0	0	0	0	0	0	0	0	0	0
Redington Twp.	3	0	0	0	0	0	0	0	0	3
Riley TWP	0	0	0	0	0	0	0	0	0	0
Sandy River Plt.	0	1	3	0	0	0	0	0	0	4
Shawtown Twp.	0	0	2	0	0	0	1	0	0	3
T1 R10 Wels	0	0	0	0	0	0	0	0	0	0
T1 R11 Wels	0	0	1	0	0	1	0	0	0	2
T2 R10 Wels	20	0	1	0	0	0	0	2	1	24
T3 R10 Wels	0	0	0	0	0	0	0	0	0	0
T7 R9 Nwp.	0	0	0	0	0	0	2	0	0	2
TA R10 Wels	38	0	0	0	0	0	4	0	2	44
TA R11 Wels	0	0	0	0	0	0	0	0	0	0
TB R11 Wels	0	0	0	0	0	0	6	0	0	6
The Forks Plt.	0	0	2	0	0	1	0	0	0	3
Township C	8	1	0	4	0	0	0	3	1	17
Township D	2	0	0	0	0	0	0	0	0	2
Township E	0	0	0	0	0	0	0	0	0	0
Wyman Twp.	1	0	0	2	0	0	0	0	0	3
Total	167	6	25	17	0	17	49	10	11	302

All other furbearers in Maine are thought to have stable and sustainable populations. The A.T., in Maine, provides excellent habitat for marten because of the large areas of spruce, fir and pine tree stands that provide these animals with food and cover.

Literature Cited

Barbour, R.W. and W.H. Davis. 1969. Bats of America. University Press of Kentucky, Lexington, KY.

Buech, R. R., R. M. Timm, and K. Siderits. 1977. A second population of rock voles, *Microtus chrotorrhinus*, in Minnesota with comments on habitat. Canadian Field-Naturalist 91(4):413-414.

Bunnell, K.D., J.T. Flinders, and M.L. Wolfe. 2006. Potential impacts of coyotes and snowmobiles on lynx conservation in the intermountain west. Wildlife Society Bulletin. 34(3):828-838.

Carroll, C. 2007. Interacting effects of climate change, landscape conversion, and harvest on carnivore populations at the range margin: marten and lynx in the northern Appalachians. Conservation Biology. 21(4):1092-1104.

Clough, G.C., and J.J. Albright. 1987. Occurrence of the northern bog lemming, *Synaptomys borealis*, in the northeastern United States. Canadian Field Naturalist. 101:611-613.

Edwards, R. L. 1963. Observations on the small mammals of the southeastern shore of Hudson Bay. Canadian Field Naturalist 77(1):1-12.

Erdle, S.Y., and C.S. Hobson. 2001. Current status and conservation strategy for the eastern small-footed myotis (*Myotis leibii*). Natural Heritage Technical Report # 00-19. Virginia Department of Conservation and Recreation, Division of Natural Heritage, Richmond, VA. 17pp.

French, T. W., and K. L. Crowell. 1985. Distribution and status of the yellow-nosed vole and rock shrew in New York. New York Fish and Game Journal 32(1):26-40.

Fuller, A.K., D.J. Harrison, and J.H. Vashon. 2007. Winter habitat selection by Canada lynx in Maine: prey abundance or accessibility? The Journal of Wildlife Management. 71(6):1980-1986.

Healy, W. M., and R. T. Brooks. 1988. Small mammal abundance in northern hardwood stands in West Virginia. Journal of Wildlife Management 52(3):491-496.

Herrmann, H., C. West, and C. Todd. 2003. A survey of rare, threatened and endangered fauna in Maine: Northwestern Region (2002-2003). Maine Department of Inland Fisheries and Wildlife, Bangor, ME.

Hoving, C.L, R.A. Joseph, and W.B. Krohn. 2003. Recent and historical distributions of Canada lynx in Maine and the northeast. Northeastern Naturalist. 10(4):363-382.

Hoving, C.L., D.J. Harrison, W.B. Krohn, and R.A. Joseph. 2005. Broad-scale predictors of Canada lynx occurrence in eastern North America. Journal of Wildlife Management. 69(2):739-751.

Kirkland, G. L., Jr., and J. A. Hart. 1999. Recent distributional records for ten species of small mammals in Pennsylvania. Northeastern Naturalist 6(1):1-18.

Kirkland, G. L. Jr., and C. M. Knipe. 1979. The rock vole (*Microtus chrotorrhinus*) as a Transition Zone species. Canadian Field-Naturalist 93:319-321.

Kirkland, G. L., Jr., and H. M. van Deusen. 1979. The shrews of the *Sorex dispar* group: *Sorex dispar* Batchelder and *Sorex gaspensis* Anthony and Goodwin. American Museum Novitates 2675:1-21.

Layser, E. F. and T. E. Burke. 1973. The northern bog lemming and its unique habitat in northeastern Washington. Murrelet 54:7-8.

Litvaitis, J.A., and D.J. Harrison. 1989. Bobcat-coyote niche relationships during a period of coyote population increase. Canadian Journal of Zoology 67:1180-1188.

Maine Department of Inland Fisheries and Wildlife (IF&W), 2007. Fur Dealer Report Booklet. Unpublished data received from Kim Morse.

Minnesota Department of Natural Resources. 2008. DNR Garmin GPS Application. http://www.dnr.state.mn.us/mis/gis/tools/arcview/extensions/DNRGarmin/DNRGarmin.html

Osgood, W. H. 1909. Biological investigations in Alaska and Yukon Territory. North American Fauna 30. 86 pp.

Poole, K.G. 2003. A review of the Canada Lynx, *Lynx canadensis*, in Canada. The Canadian Field Naturalist.117:360-372.

Preble, E. A. 1899. Description of a new lemming mouse from the White Mountains, New Hampshire. Proceedings of the Biological Society of Washington 13:43-45.

Reichel, J.D., and S.G. Beckstrom. 1994. Northern bog lemming survey: 1993. Montana Natural Heritage Program. Helena, MT. 87pp.

Reynolds, S. 2006. Monitoring the potential impacts of a wind development site on bats in the Northeast. Journal of Wildlife Management. 70(5):1219-1227.

Roscoe, B., and C. Majka. 1976. First records of the rock vole (*Microtus chrotorrhinus*) and the Gaspé shrew (*Sorex gaspensis*) from Nova Scotia and a second record of the Thompson's pygmy shrew (*Microsorex thompsoni*) from Cape Breton Island. Canadian Field-Naturalist 90:497-498.

Scott, F. W. 1987. First record of the long-tailed shrew, *Sorex dispar*, for Nova Scotia. Canadian Field-Naturalist 101:404-407.

Slough, B.G. 1999. Characteristics of Canada lynx (*Lynx canadensis*), maternal dens and denning habitat. Canadian Field-Naturalist. 113:605-607.

Stephenson, R.O., and P. Karczmarczyk. 1989. Development of techniques for evaluating lynx population status in Alaska. P-R Report W-23-1, job 7.13. Alaska Department of Fish and Game, Juneau, AK.

Timm, R. M., L. R. Heaney, and D. D. Baird. 1977. Natural history of rock voles (*Microtus chrotorrhinus*) in Minnesota. Canadian Field-Naturalist 91:177-181.

Whitaker, J. O., Jr., and T. W. French. 1984. Foods of six species of sympatric shrews from New Brunswick. Canadian Journal of Zoology 62:622-626.

Whitaker, J. O., Jr., and R. L. Martin. 1977. Food habits of *Microtus chrotorrhinus* from New Hampshire, New York, Labrador, and Quebec. Journal of Mammalogy 58:99-100.

Wilson, C., R. E. Johnson, and J. R. Reichel. 1980. New records for the northern bog lemming in Washington. Murrelet 61(3):104-106.

Woolaver, L. G., M. F. Elderkin, and F. W. Scott. 1998. *Sorex dispar* in Nova Scotia. Northeastern Naturalist 5(4):323-330.

Wright, P. L. 1950. *Synaptomys borealis* from Glacier National Park, Montana. Journal of Mammalogy 31(4):460.

Zimmerman, G.S., and W.E. Glanz. 2000. Habitat use by bats in eastern Maine. Journal of Wildlife Management. 64(4):1032-1040.

Appendix. Location, species, sex, age, reproductive status, and morphometric data for bats captured during surveys along the Appalachian Trail, Maine, 2006.

Date	Site	State	Latitude	Longitude	Species	Sex	Age	Repro. Status	FA (mm)	Weight (g)	Time
6/23/2006	Stratton Brook	ME	45.11291	-70.35135	MYSE	M	A	NR	37.5	8.0	2245
6/23/2006	Stratton Brook	ME	45.11291	-70.35135	EPFU	M	A	NR	41.3	21.3	0005
6/23/2006	Stratton Brook	ME	45.11291	-70.35135	MYSE	M	N/A	unknown	N/A	N/A	0030
6/24/2006	Stratton Brook	ME	45.11291	-70.35135	MYSE	F	A	NR	34.2	7.4	2155
6/24/2006	Stratton Brook	ME	45.11291	-70.35135	LACI	M	A	NR	54.2	20.5	2234
6/27/2006	Stratton Brook	ME	45.11291	-70.35135	MYSE	M	A	NR	37.1	7.3	2025
6/27/2006	Stratton Brook	ME	45.11291	-70.35135	MYSE	M	A	NR	37.1	7.9	2234
7/24/2006	Bear River	ME	44.57216	-70.90553	MYSE	M	A	NR	36.6	7.6	2115
7/24/2006	Bear River	ME	44.57216	-70.90553	MYSE	M	A	NR	38.3	6.8	2130
7/24/2006	Bear River	ME	44.57216	-70.90553	LANO	M	A	NR	42.9	11.2	2130
7/24/2006	Bear River	ME	44.57216	-70.90553	LANO	M	A	NR	40.7	10.3	0045
7/25/2006	Bear River	ME	44.57216	-70.90553	MYLU	M	A	NR	38.3	7.6	N/A
7/30/2006	Rangeley	ME	44.63451	-70.56743	MYSE	M	SA	NR	35.8	6.2	2050
7/30/2006	Rangeley	ME	44.63451	-70.56743	EPFU	M	A	NR	45.0	16.2	2100
7/30/2006	Rangeley	ME	44.63451	-70.56743	MYLU	M	A	NR	36.5	6.4	2100
7/30/2006	Rangeley	ME	44.63451	-70.56743	EPFU	F	A	PL	45.1	18.9	2120
7/30/2006	Rangeley	ME	44.63451	-70.56743	MYSE	M	A	NR	36.6	9.9	2120
7/30/2006	Rangeley	ME	44.63451	-70.56743	MYLU	F	SA	NR	38.1	7.6	2121
7/30/2006	Rangeley	ME	44.63451	-70.56743	EPFU	F	A	PL	46.3	18.5	2140
7/30/2006	Rangeley	ME	44.63451	-70.56743	MYSE	M	A	NR	37.1	9.6	2140
7/30/2006	Rangeley	ME	44.63451	-70.56743	MYSE	F	A	PL	38.2	8.5	2142
7/30/2006	Rangeley	ME	44.63451	-70.56743	MYSE	M	A	NR	37.8	7.8	2155
7/30/2006	Rangeley	ME	44.63451	-70.56743	MYSE	M	A	NR	38.0	8.3	2235
7/30/2006	Rangeley	ME	44.63451	-70.56743	MYLU	M	SA	NR	38.4	6.7	2235
7/30/2006	Rangeley	ME	44.63451	-70.56743	MYSE	M	A	NR	37.7	7.5	2235
7/30/2006	Rangeley	ME	44.63451	-70.56743	MYLU	M	SA	NR	37.1	7.4	2300
7/30/2006	Rangeley	ME	44.63451	-70.56743	MYSE	M	A	NR	38.4	8.1	2300
7/30/2006	Rangeley	ME	44.63451	-70.56743	MYLU	M	A	NR	38.1	8.7	2330
7/30/2006	Rangeley	ME	44.63451	-70.56743	MYSE	M	A	NR	36.8	6.8	2330
7/30/2006	Rangeley	ME	44.63451	-70.56743	MYLU	M	SA	NR	36.5	6.9	2330
7/30/2006	Rangeley	ME	44.63451	-70.56743	MYSE	M	A	NR	35.9	6.8	2330

Appendix. Location, species, sex, age, reproductive status, and morphometric data for bats captured during surveys along the Appalachian Trail, Maine, 2006 (continued).

Date	Location	State	Latitude	Longitude	Species	Sex	Age	Repro. Status	FA (mm)	Weight (g)	Time
7/31/2006	Carriage Road	ME	45.11448	-70.19077	MYLU	M	A	NR	39.4	12.6	2115
7/31/2006	Carriage Road	ME	45.11448	-70.19077	MYLU	M	A	NR	37.4	9.0	2115
7/31/2006	Carriage Road	ME	45.11448	-70.19077	MYSE	M	A	NR	37.1	7.3	2115
7/31/2006	Carriage Road	ME	45.11448	-70.19077	MYLU	F	SA	NR	37.1	7.3	2130
7/31/2006	Carriage Road	ME	45.11448	-70.19077	MYLU	F	A	NR	39.5	7.2	2310
8/1/2006	Stony Brook Road	ME	45.07544	-70.39205	MYLU	M	A	NR	37.7	10.9	2110
8/3/2006	Barren Cliffs	ME	45.4086	-69.4157	MYLU	M	A	NR	39.2	7.3	2100
8/3/2006	Barren Cliffs	ME	45.4086	-69.4157	MYLU	F	SA	NR	38.1	7.1	2145
8/3/2006	Barren Cliffs	ME	45.4086	-69.4157	MYLU	F	SA	NR	36.0	6.2	2245
8/3/2006	Barren Cliffs	ME	45.4086	-69.4157	MYSE	M	A	NR	37.9	7.6	2320
8/3/2006	Barren Cliffs	ME	45.4086	-69.4157	MYLU	F	A	NR	37.4	6.4	0000
8/3/2006	Barren Cliffs	ME	45.4086	-69.4157	MYSE	M	A	NR	35.6	5.7	0000
8/3/2006	Barren Cliffs	ME	45.4086	-69.4157	EPFU	M	A	NR	45.5	20.0	0015
8/4/2006	Barren Cliffs	ME	45.4086	-69.4157	MYLU	M	A	NR	37.1	6.9	2100
8/4/2006	Barren Cliffs	ME	45.4086	-69.4157	MYLU	F	SA	NR	36.7	6.4	2120
8/4/2006	Barren Cliffs	ME	45.4086	-69.4157	MYLU	M	A	NR	36.9	9.6	2120
8/4/2006	Barren Cliffs	ME	45.4086	-69.4157	MYLU	M	A	NR	37.8	8.0	2120
8/4/2006	Barren Cliffs	ME	45.4086	-69.4157	MYLU	F	A	NR	38.6	8.6	2121
8/4/2006	Barren Cliffs	ME	45.4086	-69.4157	MYLU	M	A	NR	38.3	7.2	2135
8/4/2006	Barren Cliffs	ME	45.4086	-69.4157	MYLU	M	A	NR	37.7	6.8	2245
8/4/2006	Barren Cliffs	ME	45.4086	-69.4157	MYLU	M	A	NR	38.2	6.2	2245
8/4/2006	Barren Cliffs	ME	45.4086	-69.4157	MYLU	F	A	NR	37.2	8.0	2245
8/4/2006	Barren Cliffs	ME	45.4086	-69.4157	MYLU	M	SA	NR	36.6	6.7	2315
8/4/2006	Barren Cliffs	ME	45.4086	-69.4157	MYSE	F	A	NR	36.3	6.7	2331
8/4/2006	Barren Cliffs	ME	45.4086	-69.4157	MYLU	M	SA	NR	37.6	9.1	0002
8/4/2006	Barren Cliffs	ME	45.4086	-69.4157	MYLU	M	A	NR	37.1	6.7	N/A
8/7/2006	Crocker Cirque	ME	45.03942	-70.3446	LABO	N/A	N/A	unknown	0.0	0.0	2110
8/7/2006	Crocker Cirque	ME	45.03942	-70.3446	MYSE	F	A	NR	38.2	7.0	2110
8/7/2006	Crocker Cirque	ME	45.03942	-70.3446	MYLU	F	A	NR	39.6	9.0	2135
8/7/2006	Crocker Cirque	ME	45.03942	-70.3446	MYLU	M	SA	NR	38.8	7.8	2135
8/7/2006	Crocker Cirque	ME	45.03942	-70.3446	MYSE	M	A	NR	36.0	6.3	2135
8/7/2006	Crocker Cirque	ME	45.03942	-70.3446	MYLU	M	SA	NR	38.0	6.8	2200
8/7/2006	Crocker Cirque	ME	45.03942	-70.3446	MYLU	F	SA	NR	39.1	7.3	2200
8/7/2006	Crocker Cirque	ME	45.03942	-70.3446	MYLU	F	SA	NR	39.1	7.5	2200

Appendix. Location, species, sex, age, reproductive status, and morphometric data for bats captured during surveys along the Appalachian Trail, Maine, 2006 (continued).

Date	Location	State	Latitude	Longitude	Species	Sex	Age	Repro. Status	FA (mm)	Weight (g)	Time
8/7/2006	Crocker Cirque	ME	45.03942	-70.3446	MYLU	F	SA	NR	37.0	7.9	2200
8/7/2006	Crocker Cirque	ME	45.03942	-70.3446	MYLU	M	SA	NR	36.9	6.2	2230
8/7/2006	Crocker Cirque	ME	45.03942	-70.3446	MYLU	F	SA	NR	39.3	7.5	2230
8/7/2006	Crocker Cirque	ME	45.03942	-70.3446	MYLU	F	SA	NR	38.2	6.7	2300
8/7/2006	Crocker Cirque	ME	45.03942	-70.3446	MYLU	F	A	PL	38.6	7.1	2325
8/7/2006	Crocker Cirque	ME	45.03942	-70.3446	MYLU	M	A	unknown	37.5	7.1	2325

KEY
Species: MYLU=little brown bat; MYSE=northern long-eared bat; EPFU=big brown bat; LABO=red bat; LANO=silver-haired bat; LACI=hoary bat
Sex: M=Male; F=Female; N/A=Not Available
Age: A=Adult; SA=Subadult
Repro. Status: PL= Post Lactating; NR= Non-reproductive
FA: Length of forearm

The Department of the Interior protects and manages the nation's natural resources and cultural heritage; provides scientific and other information about those resources; and honors its special responsibilities to American Indians, Alaska Natives, and affiliated Island Communities.

NPS 962/101073 February 2010

www.ingramcontent.com/pod-product-compliance
Lightning Source LLC
Chambersburg PA
CBHW080907290526
45795CB00007BA/2439